Forget Me Knots

by Karl Rohnke

Illustrated by Plynn Williams

KENDALL/HUNT PUBLISHING COMPANY
4050 Westmark Drive Dubuque, Iowa 52002

ISBN 0-8403-7138-1

Printed in the United States of America
10 9 8 7 6 5 4 3 2

Knots to You...

Writing books is fun: organizing and formating the raw material isn't. I'm very appreciative of those people who have helped me get this book from the screen to the printed page: **Bonnie Hannable**, **Tom Zierk**, **Mary Henton**, **Bob Ryan**, **Conrad Willeman**.

Dave Klim, as always, has been dependably available whenever I needed someone to help me set up or to pose for a needed photograph.

Particular thanks to **Plynn Williams** for his skill and patience in dealing with the interminable changes that inevitably occur when trying to make a technical subject understandable. Plynn and I planned this book together over ten years ago, so it's particularly satisfying to have shared our skills in bringing that initial idea to fruition. The 9:00 AM in-house meetings over coffee and various homemade goodies will be sorely missed.

Contents

Preface

I like knots. I like knot books. I have at least a half dozen of these cordage primers shoved into various bookshelves around the house, and I am comforted that they are there to save me from "never not knowing" a knot when the time comes. Even though I know, when the time comes, I'll revert to one of the old reliables (bowline, figure eight loop, half hitch, etc.) rather than researching just the right knot, bend or hitch. But there is satisfation in knowing that almost every bend and lay of rope ever invented and recorded is within easy reach... even if I don't want or need that specific knot.

The Ashley Book of Knots (610 pages, 7,000 drawings, over 3,900 knots) is a well-known and voluminous research source, and particularly useful if you are trying to learn how to coachwhip an eye or throw a french cringle. But post-participants in Adventure workshops are usually scrambing (1st period, D block) to remember the twists and turns of the basic bowline and could care less about the aesthetics of seven-strand sinnets. In keeping with this sense of program specificity, the contents of *Forget Me Knots* pertain only to ropes course-related activities.

Plynn Williams, the talented commercial artist who has created the illustrations for many other PA publications, has turned his artist's eye toward "freezing" the rope in a most revealing and multi-dimentional way. Following his clearly defined sight-sequences in combination with a few photos and the descriptive text should get you through the not-so-complex knot configurations that you ***need to know***. As I've often said to knot novices, "learning to tie a particular knot is not like learning how to ride a bike." Once on a bike, balanced and moving, the essential riding skill becomes ingrained even if you don't ride again for years. In contrast, if a knot is initially learned and not practiced, it will have slipped from your memory banks by next Wednesday. So here's a specific reader-friendly reference that will show-and-tell you how to tighten a fidget ladder or fashion a Studebaker Wrap, in addition to clearly reviewing the more classic knot sequences.

I've been perusing quite a few knot books during the last six months, trying to make sure that I'm not flagarently flaunting accepted tying techniques or debunking cordage icons. I found a couple things I have been doing over the years that probably could be presented better (Ref. tying a left-handed bowline), but I have consistently tried to pass along the most accepted rope techniques. I have also included a generally frowned on knot application (Ref. using a square knot for a swiss seat tie-off) in order to streamline the curriculum and involve more students on a per day basis. Check what I have to say in the text before you make up your mind.

Introduction

Knot — "Any complication in rope except accidental ones."

Clifford Ashley

Forget me knots? Sure, that's why you purchased the book, right? Flat-out forgot the bowline, *and* on-a-bight...even the reef knot? Oh boy, you do need help! And help's here, without a lot of other Adventure stuff in the way to impede your steel-trap memory mechanism and subtract from the pedagogic pureness of your intent: Yeah...sure!

Forget Me Knots is a reference book pertaining to cordage specifics; i.e., the knots and bends herein pertain and apply to ropes course use only. That's not to say you won't find other uses for these knot sequences, but the difference between this modest collection and Ashley's famous knot anthology is about 3,875 knots and 600+ pages, plus the comfort of knowing that what you are trying to remember was once part of your performing repertoire (Adventure Programming Workshop; Day 2), and that each knot has an essential curriculum use.

There are no six-strand sinnets or dog-bolter knots here, partly because I don't know what they are or how to tie them, but mostly because their application is beyond the pale of ropes course use. Also, this pocket-sized book doesn't deal with cosmetic twists and turns that don't secure, tighten, or protect anything. No padding here — this book is *PURE FUNCTION...* and some essential fooling around, of course.

In past Project Adventure workshops, I have talked about the need to establish yourself as an expert with knots. ("An ounce of image is worth a pound of performance.") However,

being an expert doesn't mean that you have to know ump-teen knots and how to apply them. My suggestion referred to learning a couple more knots than were necessary to teach — so that the students think you are familiar with every knot that has ever been tied — and to know those couple of knots well... real well. Nothing engenders a feeling of trust more than a genuinely adept presentation and display of what you are trying to teach. Hit 'em with some basic rope terminology (glossary) and then demonstrate the knot with confidence. Tying a bend or hitch rapidly isn't necessary (counterproductive actually), but a digital display of casual confidence will do a lot toward developing trust in you as THE instructor. Convince them that this knot sequence is part of your life style, that you tie it regularly and use it without hesitation. People are often leery of *serious* knots because of war stories they hear about bends and hitches coming undone at critical times resulting in property loss or personal disasters. Tell them and show them that your knots don't slip or come undone if tied the way you are about to expertly show them. Then demonstrate a chosen knot without hesitation or flaw in the tying process. If you mess up the sequence, you are compromising the

group's conceptual trust in you, and ostensibly your ability to keep them safe. Don't minimize the security factor that you provide for a beginning student during the initial learning process of climbing, rappelling, etc. If you doubt how much impact your words and presence can affect beginners, watch novice rappellers' eyes as they approach "the big step." Their gaze will be riveted on *you*, looking for the reassurance that everything is OK. Don't pretend to be an expert — become one and earn that trust. You don't have to climb at a 5.11 degree of difficulty, or be a climber at all, but you do have to know what you are talking about and be able to display an expert's adeptness with a few technical skills in order to gain the trust of the students and promote their willingness to learn potentially scary material.

On the positive side, when you tell the students that they will be tying their own protection knots, limited attention span is seldom a problem. Every potential climber wants to know the *EXACT* and *PERFECT* way to tie *HIS/HER* knot. Emphasize checking each others' knots, indicating that this visual check builds trust, reinforces what a correct knot sequence looks like, and increases the safety factor for the entire group.

Now that you have everyone seriously involved in cordage manipulation, and in tune with the gravity of the situation (yes indeed, that was a pun), lighten up a bit by introducing a couple nonsense knots. After the students have had a chance to learn and practice two or three essential knots, offer an attractive trick knot sequence for them to learn, "...if they want to." *Nonsense Knots* should always be optional, but be offered in such an attractive or bizarre manner that they all want to practice the sequence in order to fool their friends or simply to please themselves. Sometimes as the result of being genetically fumble-fingered or becoming up-tight because "...your life depends on that knot," some students will dismiss the whole rope/knot process out-of-hand and give up trying or even avoid beginning. Make the hands-on process fun again by demonstrating *the world's fastest bowline*, or trick them out of their socks by, *threading the needle.* Attempt to make "knots" a good time for them and you'll enjoy it also. (See pages 14–22.)

The format of this knotty book, as you can see, includes photographs and illustrations to bolster the text. Subjecting a hands-on (and sometimes reluctant) learner to pure text is a cruel joke, and guarantees lots of unused books. So if you get stuck in conTEXT, refer to the more visual parts of the pages.

The Knots

Where do we start? With a simple bend to bolster your confidence? A basic hitch to jog your memory? Nah, let's go for one of the biggies (bowline-on-a-bight), because that's the one you told yourself you would NEVER forget. Never in this case measured about a fortnight.

Bowline on-a-Bight

*"If you can't remember how to tie the bowline, tie **lots** of what you do remember."*

Relax, this is not a hard knot to tie, and after all, what I'm about to tell you and the illustrations that you are perusing are all stuff you have seen before: the following text material is just a bit of review. I'm going to talk you through the knot, just like on day two of the workshop. Look at the illustrations and photographs 'twixt glances at the text. Also, if in doubt, check the glossary, 'cause I'm going to use rope talk; can't tell your bight from a loop otherwise, then where would you be?

Get yourself a 10'–12' length of retired kernmantle rope for practice knotting, and fashion an open loop near the end of the rope. The working end, past the loop, should be at least three feet long. Using the double line loop as a single piece, tie a loose overhand knot. You DO remember the overhand I hope. If not ...*sigh*...take a look at the illustration on this page. (While you are reviewing the overhand, check out the small star that appears in each drawing; it's there to help you visually sequence the illustrations.) Hold the loosely-tied overhand knot in the palm of your left hand so that the loop (tongue) points toward you. Pass your right hand up through the tongue loop from underneath (#1a). This next bit of text requires that you look at the illustration carefully.

#1a

With your hand through the loop from below, and using your thumb and forefinger as pincers, grasp the two sections of rope that make up the far top portion of the overhand knot (#1b). ***Stop Reading and Look!*** Using your free left hand grasp the tip of the tongue loop that's around your wrist and bring it down over your hand and past your fingers with a **tug**; i.e., forcefully (#1c, d).

#1b

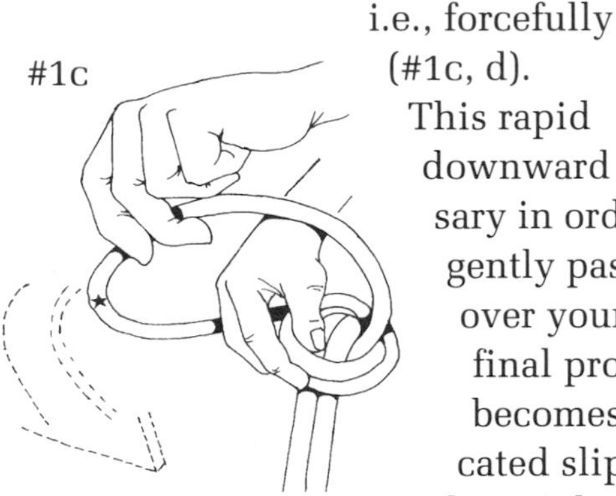

#1c

This rapid downward jerking movement is necessary in order to form the knot. If you gently pass the loop over your hand, the final product often becomes a complicated slip knot. Still doesn't look like much, eh? Take a closer look because the knot is already tied — surprise! Now all you have to do is "dress it up." The longish tongue needs to be drawn up tight to the main part of the knot. Visually follow the two sections of rope that constitute the tongue up to the body of the knot.

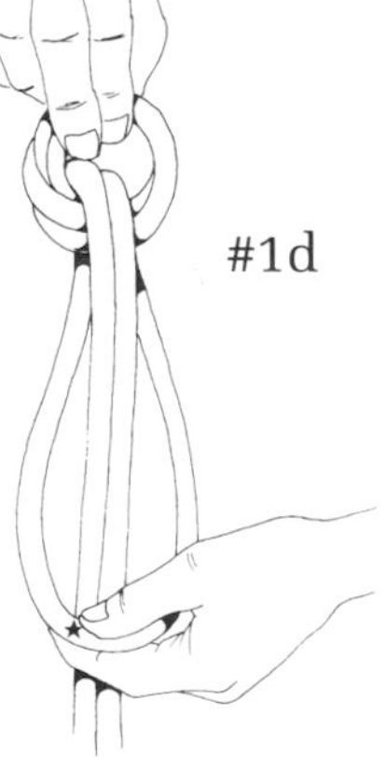

#1d

Hold the body of the knot in your left hand and pull the continuation of these two tongue sections up with the right hand, until the bottom of the tongue comes up snug against the formed knot (#1e, f). What you are holding is a bowline-on-a-bight, tied and dressed. Remember now? No problem. Can't stop there, though. Every climbing knot used on a ropes course needs to be backed up with a safety knot.

#1e

#1f

Although the primary knot (bowline on-a-bight in this case) is an excellent bend of rope, this knot tied in synthetic rope — with enough climbing movement and manipulation — could work itself free. So, to make me happy, to please the parents, to assuage the administration's fears and to provide personal peace of mind, learn this back-up sequence and use it every time you tie a knot that involves someone's safety — including your own.

#2a

Grip the just-tied knot in your hand, palm-down, so that the working end of the rope comes out of your fist on the same side as your thumb (#2a). Grasp the working end (which should measures at least 16") with your other hand and wrap it around your thumb twice, making sure that the second wrap is made toward the hand, not toward the tip of the thumb, and causing the rope to cross itself (#2b).

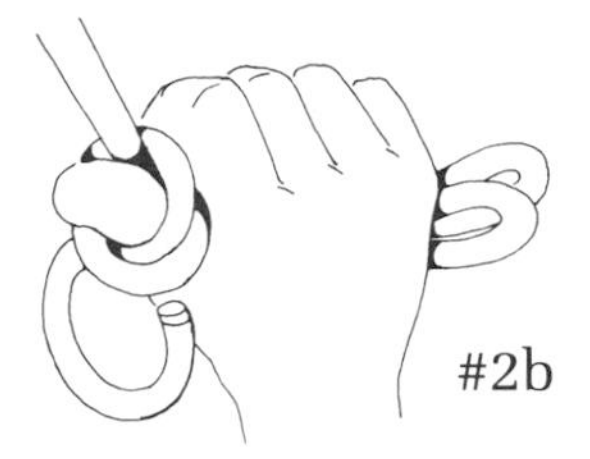
#2b

Continue as if to complete a third wrap, but remove your thumb from the double wrap ("tunnel") and insert (reeve) the working rope end through this tunnel so that the rope end moves away from your hand (#2c)

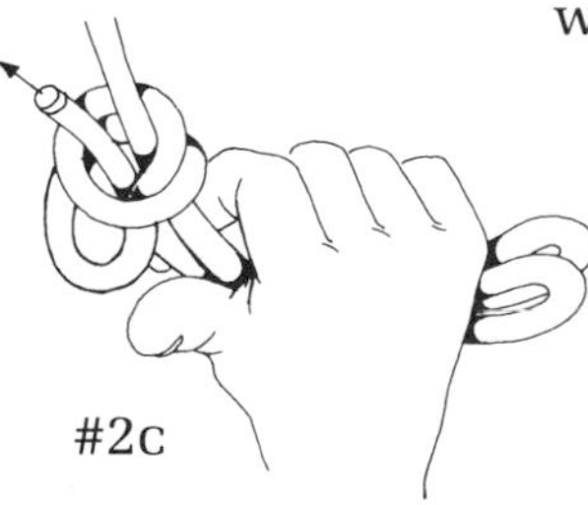
#2c

Adjust this tunnel safety knot so that it tightens and is positioned immediately beneath the primary knot that it is protecting; i.e., don't tighten it up three inches below the main knot. If you have too much working end remaining, complete one or two additional wraps around your thumb before reeving the end through the tunnel. You should leave at least 3" of working end as a minimum. (See photos of *bowline on-a-bight* and *figure eight loop* under **Knot Application.**)

The safety knot that you just completed tying is actually one-half of a Double Fisherman's knot. If you had started with two overlapping rope ends opposed (#3) and tied a tunnel knot (as above) with each working end, you would have fashioned

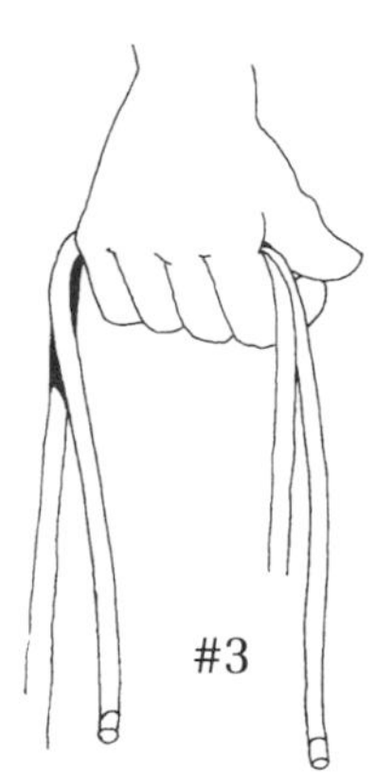
#3

an excellent means of securing two ropes of equal diameter together. The only drawback to the Double Fisherman's knot is its tendency to jam under pressure, becoming extremely difficult to untie. If I knew beforehand that the tied rope ends were going to be subjected to a strong pull, I would probably secure the working ends together with a bowline tied into a bowline (#4).

Bowline Around an Object

The bowline on-a-bight is a fine mid-rope knot and for ropes course application also functions well as a rope end double loop knot for attaching a climbing rope (via a carabiner) to a pelvic wrap arrangement, but if you need a knot sequence that will allow you to tie a rope end around an object (tree, person, car bumper), here 'tis.

#4

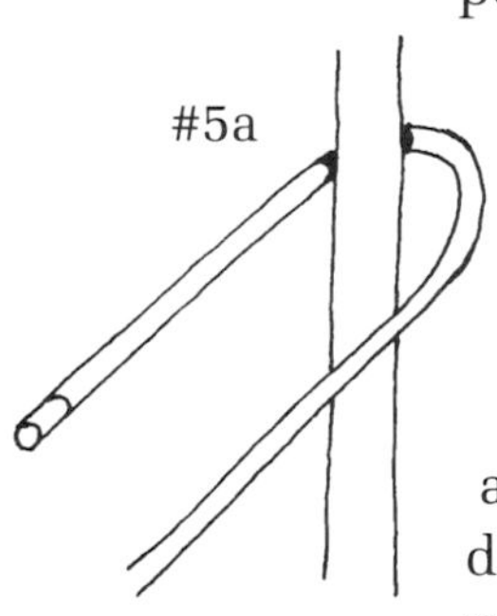
#5a

Everyone seems to have a favorite way to tie a bowline, and I'm not so presumptuous as to think that my way is the best; but we have been teaching this following technique successfully at Project Adventure workshops for nearly twenty years; so why not humor me and give it a try? If you like it, it's yours. If you don't like it, keep tying it your old way: no worries. It's the final knot that counts; how you get there is pure preference.

Pass the working end of the rope around the object that you want to encircle (say, a tree). If you are right-handed, the standing part of the rope should be in your right hand and the working end in your left hand (#5a). Note to left-handed folk: All the tying instructions in this book are for right-handed people — majority rules kind of thing. To

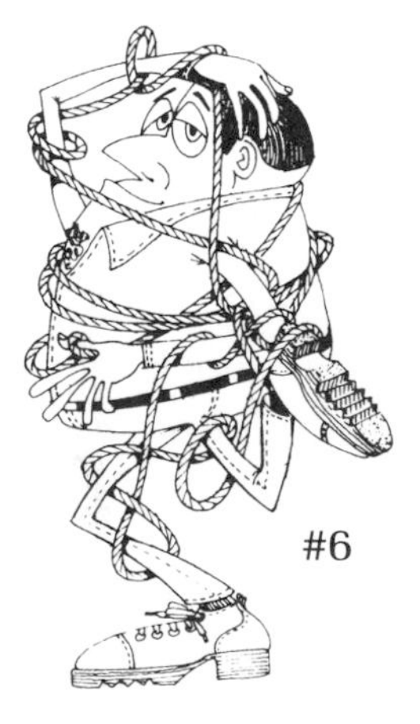
#6

establish a consistent right/left alignment, mentally shift the instructions so that vise versa puts the rope and text into reverse. What? (#6)

Make an overhand loop in the standing part of the rope, so that the loop is located about 12" from the object that you are tying the rope around. Make sure that you form an overhand loop, not an underhand loop (#5b).

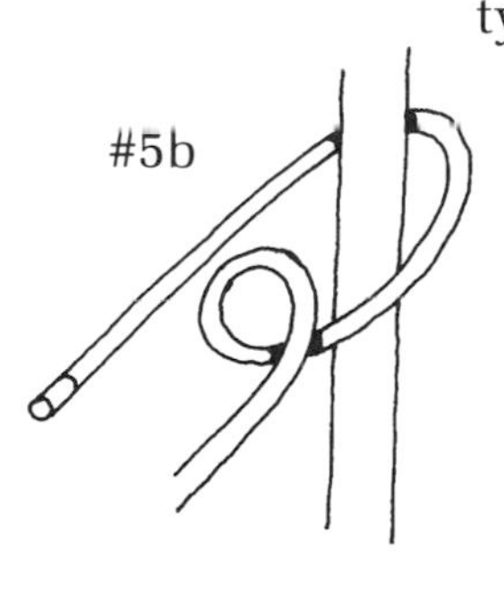

Feed a bight section of the rope's standing part from below, up and through the overhand loop, establishing a slip knot. Pinch this slippery knot between your thumb and forefinger, as in the illustration, to temporarily maintain the knot's form (#5c).

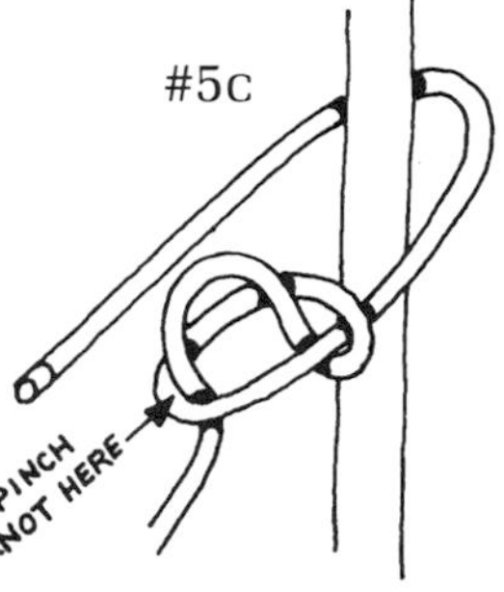

Reeve the working end of the rope (the section in your left hand) through the bight loop established in the slip knot. It doesn't make a lot of difference in which direction the rope is reeved, but it's reported that you will get a slightly stronger (maybe 5%) final bowline knot if you reeve the rope end through the loop away from yourself (#5d). You should now be again holding the working end in your left hand, as you begin to pull with your right hand on the standing part. (Just HOLD with the left hand, don't pull.) Continue to pull with the right hand until the knot starts to form. The bowline knot will often form itself as the result of this gentle pulling. If it doesn't, put your left thumb (yes, you can let go of the working end) on that portion of the developing knot as indicated in the illustration, and push convincingly, while you continue to pull with the right hand (#5e)

#5d

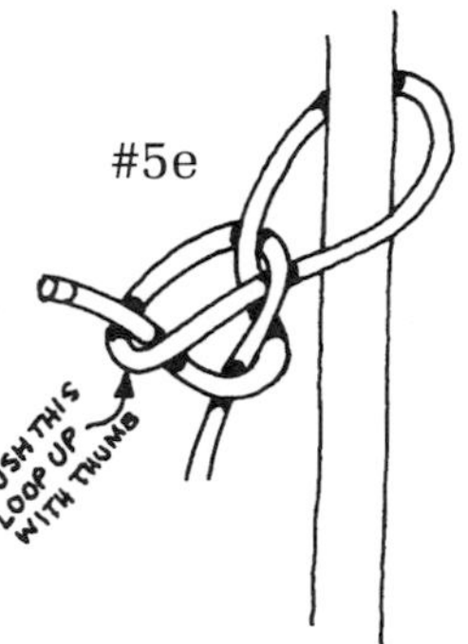

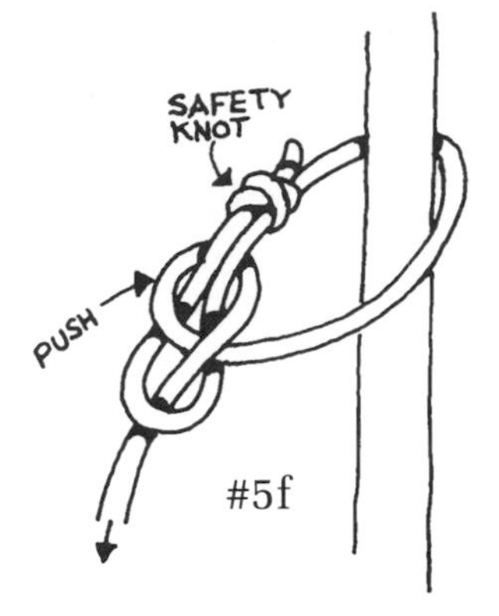

#5f

Continue pulling on the standing part, and there's your bowline knot. Is that slick, or what? I really like this knot sequence; lots of image and a solid final bend of rope. Don't forget to tie a safety knot with the working end of the rope: bowlines are notorious for working themselves free (#5f).

If you know that this bowline knot and loop are going to withstand a particularly hard pull, pass a loop of rope around the tree before you tie the knot. This is called a bowline on-a-round-turn (#7). The round-turn takes a considerable amount of strain off the knot. Do not take a round-turn on a portion of the human anatomy. A tree trunk can put up with the rope squeeze produced, our pliant and yielding bods cannot.

See, your fears were foundless. There you are, bowline in hand without so much as a fumbled finger or having to remember which way the rabbit went into the hole, while he was scratching his stomach, or breaking the glass while going around the tree...or something. Memorizing a limmerick or inane ditty that involves furry animals in order to remember rope positioning or sequence is counterproductive, because if you forget the rhyme, the knot synapses disappear also.

BOWLINE ON A ROUNDTURN
#7

Now that you know how to tie a couple knots of this genre, you better learn how to pronounce them; can't have you go around saying bow (opposite of curtsy: first half of bow-wow) line. It's bow (bow tie) lin (lin-seed oil), with the accent on the bow. Try beau-lyn. Blame it on long-dead sailors, it's not my idea.

Bowline on-a-bight, bowline around an object, bowline on-a-round-turn, bowline tied into a bowline, and finally the "king of knots," the bowline itself. Up to this point we have been

dealing with variations of the basic bowline, but have not talked about or illustrated the bowline that produces a simple loop. Now the good news: you don't need it. If you can tie all the bowline variations covered so far, you won't need the single loop bowline for any ropes course application. *Pause for predictable reader response...*OK, OK, we'll do it. I knew I wouldn't get away without at least referring to the basic bowline, being the **King of Knots**, and all...So, I asked Plynn to dynamically demonstrate the visual kinetics of tying a bowline via the old flying cartoon technique (Mickey Mouse, Popeye, et. al.).

If you haven't already, use your thumb to flip through the page-top portion of this book. Watch the separate drawings merge into a rapid-fire representation of the single bowline tying sequence and the timber hitch/half hitch hauling combo. Kinda fun, eh? Try flipping the pages in reverse. Try flipping them any way you want, it's your book.

And now, having taxed ourselves to the max with the bowline family of knots, let's tie a truly easy knot; the figure eight loop.

Figure Eight Loop

When I'm teaching this simple knot (also called figure eight on-a-bight) to an "on-sight" group, I'll instruct them to just watch the tying procedure a couple times before attempting to reproduce what I'm demonstrating: it's that kind of visual knot. I'll silently and slowly tie and untie the knot perhaps 3–4 times, offering no verbal back-up. My suggestion to them is to try manipulating the knot whenever they feel ready, and then to help others as soon as they feel comfortable with the sequence. Encourage students to help one another with knot tying. This type of spontaneous cooperation will help reduce cordage confusion, establish trust among group members, and reduce your teaching load.

In keeping with an eyes-only approach, take a look at the sequential illustrations and give it a try (#8a–d). If you don't twist the rope enough before reeving the bight loop through the formed loop you will end up with an overhand loop: not good. If you twist the rope too much you will end up with a stevedore's knot: not bad. Any one of the three knots (overhand loop, figure eight loop, or stevedore's knot) provides a secure loop, but the overhand, under tension, can jam tight; well beyond your teeth and fingernail's ability to loosen it. But that's not all bad, 'cause now you can swiftly and surely reach for your holstered, folding, lock-back, 6" Damascus carbon-steel blade and slash that Gordian imitation to cowstails and fibers. I LOVE knots that won't come undone... but enough of this cut and slash fun...

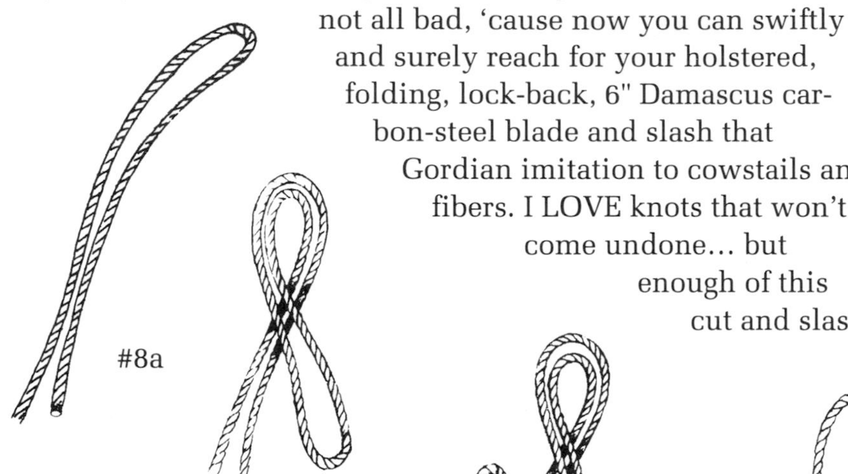

Take a look at your figure eight loop. Does it look like a figure eight (#8e)? If so, you have it. If not, look at the illustration and try again. Put your knife away!

If you are going to use this end loop as a substitute for the bowline on-a-bight, don't forget to tie on a tunnel safety knot with what's left of the working end. If you do not have enough working end left to tie a double turn safety knot with a few inches of working end remaining, undo the whole thing and begin again — it's not worth fooling around with, and you'll feel better with a well-tied safety knot.

Safety knot this, and safety knot that; after awhile the students get tired of hearing it and treat your admonitions like all parental-type "be careful" comments that are offered in good faith, but are mostly an I-told-you-so afterthought.

#8e

Show the students how easily a square knot can dissolve to nothing if safety knots are lacking. It's a grand and impressive display of knot knowledge and usually causes your novice knotters to become wide-eyed aware of safety knot function.

Plynn's cartoon illustration says it all, but to fulfill an author's knee-jerk sense of rhetorical responsibility, do this. Tie a square knot (reef knot, thumb knot, package knot — all the same) using two ends of 3/8"–1/2" rope: kernmantle works best if you have it. With the knot displayed in front of you, hold onto the right standing part with your right hand. Grasp the right working end with your left hand and pull that end sharply to the left (#9a). This single jerking movement will cause the square knot to dissolve into a

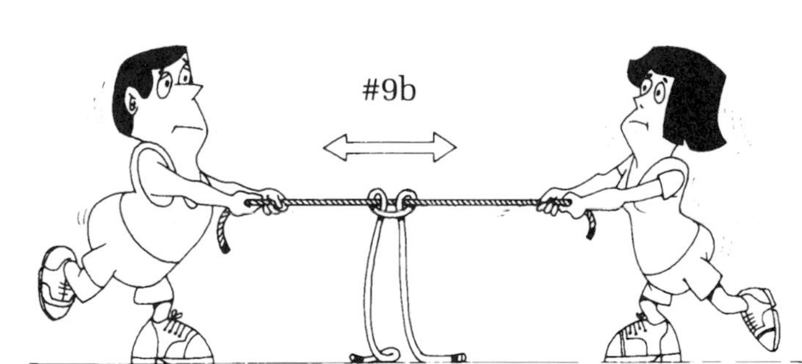

lark's head knot, also called a cow hitch or girth hitch (#9b). The lark's head, although a fine knot (hitch) for many applications, will not hold a falling climber or a falling anything. Still holding the standing part with your right hand, use the fingers of your left hand to encircle the rope and slide the lark's head completely off the rope. You can add a smidgen of drama to this fractured moment by pointedly screaming (Aaaaargh!) as the now disfigured body of the lark's head knot flies off the end of the rope. Admonishing students to "tie your safety knots" is soon met with knowing nods of compliance, rather than macabre jokes and hoots of indifference.

The square knot is very easy to tie, and that's why we use it programmatically. Compared to other knots used to join (bend) two ropes or webbing ends together, it is not a great knot, in fact it's inferior in just about every facet, except ease of tying. Remember tho', the large majority of students you are working with are not going to pursue rock climbing as a sport and could care less what kind of knot they are being taught as long as it's easy to tie and supports them without fail. The square knot is a breeze for them to learn, and is made safe by the addition of a safety knot tied with each working end; i.e., two tunnel knots, one on each side. Even the dreaded granny knot (a square knot tied asymmetrically) is okay to use IF safety knots are applied to either side. If you are infatuated or occupationally ingrained with other attaching types of knots (frost knot, water knot, bowline) use them. No worries. I'm just passing along what Project Adventure is and has been doing for the past twenty years.

Nonsense Knots

Nonsense knots (as referred to earlier in the text) are those non-essential twists and turns of rope and strand used by that wisest of teachers who recognizes learning enjoyment as the key to responsive beginning and long-term remembering. I'll remember a knot that will "save my life" for as long as my life is remotely threatened, but give me a knot that I can enjoy and use to amaze my friends, and I'll not only learn it with alacrity, but remember its patterns and purpose well beyond its indicated lack of program significance. A bowline bend has a variety of utilitarian purposes, but it's a need-to-know knot, and therefore should be approached academically and with purpose. *Puppy Knots; Thread the Needle; Tug Boat Bowline,* are knots that exist because someone had a sense of cordage humor and a keen capacity for play. The reward for tying a nonsense knot is the fun along the way and the visual end result that may mystify your impromptu audience or simply make you feel like you did something unique. Here, try one. Spontaneous folderol can be good for you; like cholesterol pills aren't.

Tugboat Bowline a.k.a. The John Wayne Bowline

Sometimes referred to as "The world's fastest bowline."

I have always disagreed with the teaching technique (win/lose competition) of having students tie knots for speed, feeling that a well-tied knot is inherently safer than a quick one. But, I don't deny that tying a knot efficiently is satisfying, so ready yourself for the height of efficiency. The Tugboat Bowline knot sequence, when first performed, is SO fast that you may tie it and untie it before you knew it was tied in the first place. That last bit of ambiguity refers to a flying knot error that occurs with some frequency while learning this knot. Handled with panache, the error can become a "...want to see it again?" statement of supreme confidence. You will know what I'm referring to as you make your first few attempts.

Use a supple rope (kernmantle) for this "knot throwing." Hard lay rope, such as Skyline, does not allow the formation of the knot at a speed that makes the trick satisfying. After all, if you don't look good while tying the knot, what's the use?

Take a look at these sequenced photographs that depict this ersatz bowline's dynamic tying sequence. Things to remember as you try to keep from slapping the rope into your crotch:

- There should be at least 18" of working rope end held beyond your throwing hand (the right hand in the photos).
- Hold everything well in front of you when you "throw" the working end to prevent whipping yourself in the groin: not cool and significantly painful.
- After the throw, put what's in your right hand through the loop held in your left hand.
- Pull the right-handed material up and through the loop with the left hand, while pulling down on the standing part with the right hand. This action will either form and tighten the knot, or if your initial throwing length was too short, will result in a grand display of absolutely nothing. Kind of funny the first time, but somewhat tedious to watch if repeated over and over. Remember...*with panache*!
- Punctuating your display of knot-tying speed and nimble-fingered legerdemain with a terminating shout can add to the drama and impressiveness of your rapid manipulations.

Beware, if indeed you do "miss" the knot, that your macro display of flying ropes, emphasized by an ebullient shout, will result in a less-than-impressive finale.

Warning — The *Tugboat Bowline* as depicted is NOT a true bowline and should not be used for any ropes course or climbing situation where a person's safety is involved.

If you feel that you HAVE to introduce a knot-tying race, use the Tugboat Bowline as the vehicle and end result; it's designed for speed of tying. Occasional whacks and slaps to the anatomical nether-land or complete kinesthetic screw-ups nicely reduce the potential seriousness of one-on-one competition.

If you want to try knot-racing with a more familiar bend, ask your students to stick out a foot or two and see how fast they can tie a bow-knot in their shoe laces. I think you will be amazed and surprised at how many different tying styles you will witness. The *bunny ears* technique is by far my favorite

Tugboat Bowline Sequence

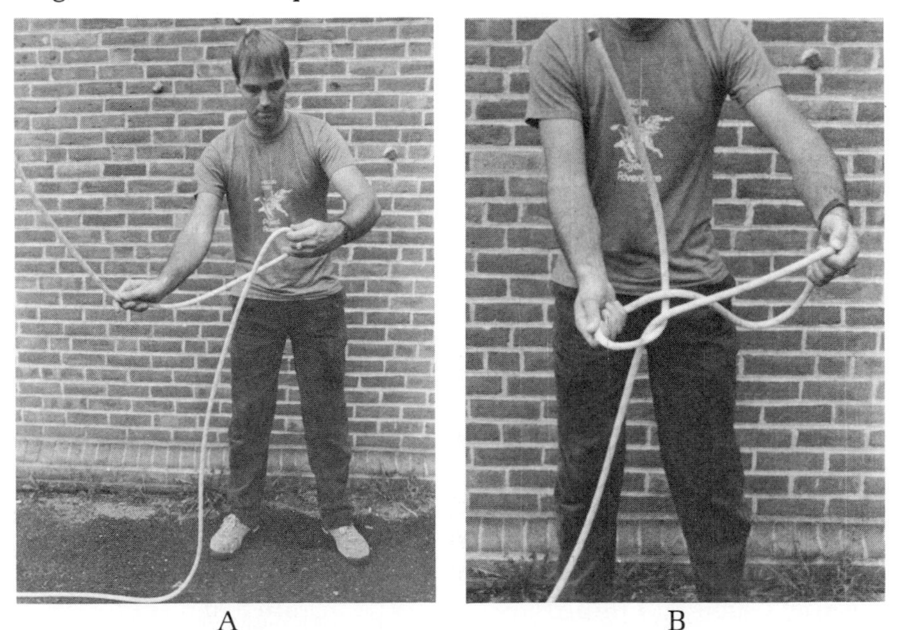

A B

digital display, but is by no means the speediest: The *New Jersey overlap* method maintains that distinction.

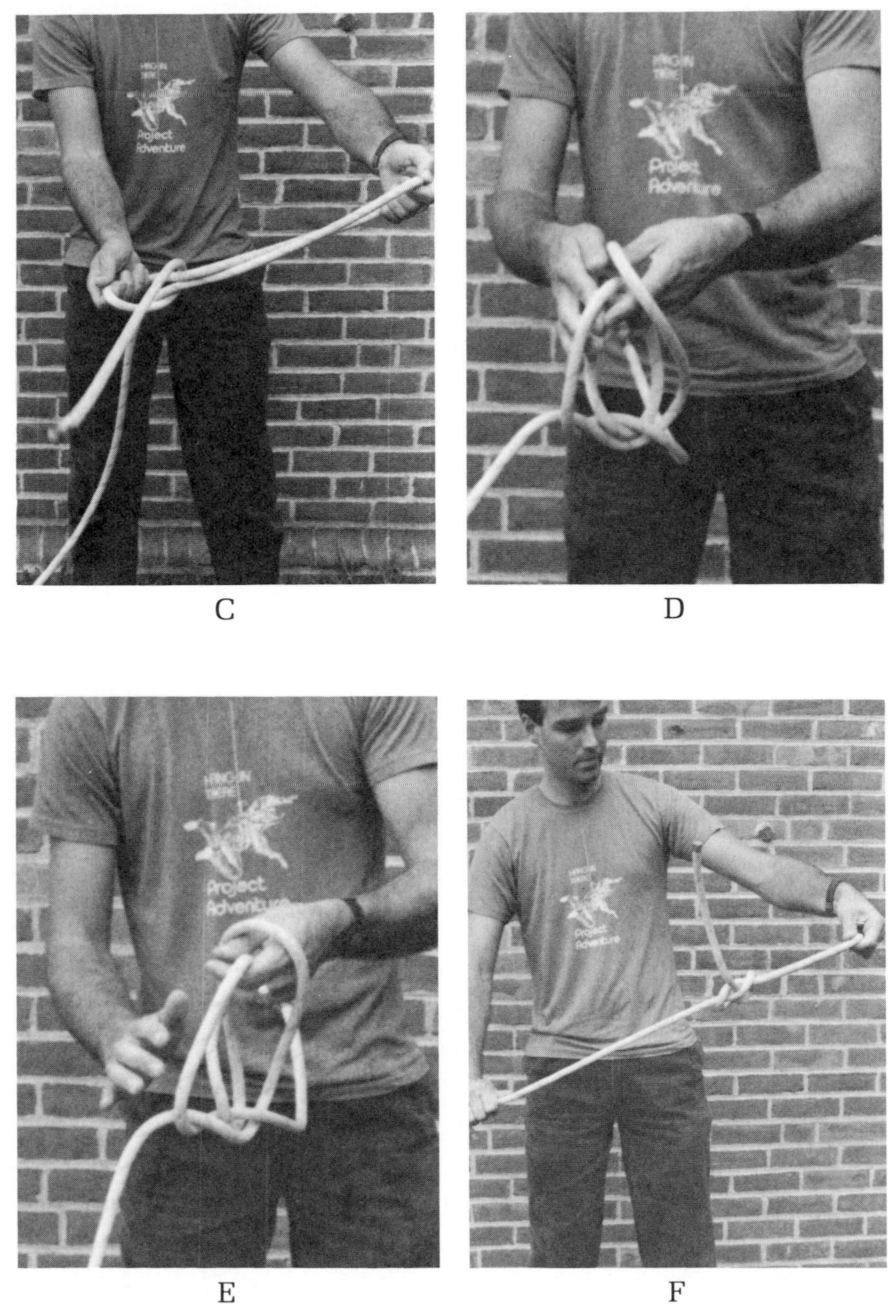

C D

E F

Thread the Needle

#10a

Threading the Needle is perhaps the most improbable of the various nonsense knots, and is also the most difficult to master. Notice I said, MASTER. This is a sequence that you don't just DO, you perform it with élan and a prestidigitatious flair.

The boastful preliminary to this explosive bit of legardemain, is to convince your audience that you can pass a section of working rope end *through* a hand-held loop faster than their eyes can follow. And indeed, by flamboyantly demonstrating what they don't believe is happening, your boast seems to fulfill itself, but, as we wizards of rope manipulation know, the hand *is* quicker than the eye. It requires a bit of showmanship to make this "trick" work, but after a couple rapid reevings, you will have convinced your audience that they have just observed the "world's fastest hands."

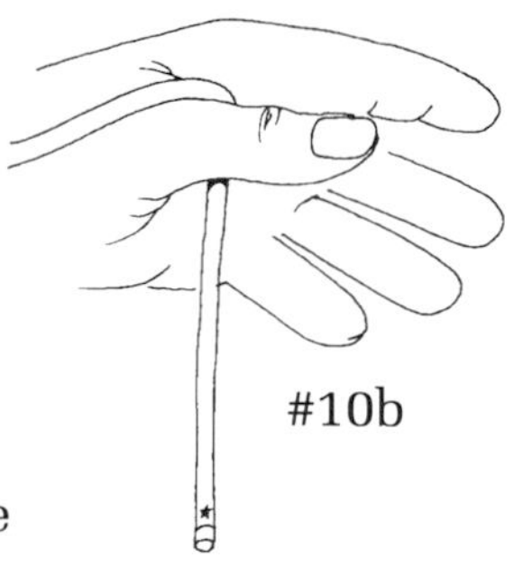

#10b

Follow the illustrations and proceed slowly in order to "see" the sequence that must occur for the trick to work. ***Trick?*** Ah yes... sorry, but you don't have the world's fastest hands, just the trickiest. As you form the loop, be sure to twist the standing end *away* from your body, then tuck it *under* the last turn coming off your your thumb (the standing end of the loop is nearest to your wrist—#10d). The rope end marked with a small star in the illustrations is the end you supposedly manipulate through the formed loop. The trick depends on actually missing the loop, and letting the trailing rope slide under your thumb (10e) until it ends up "through" the loop.

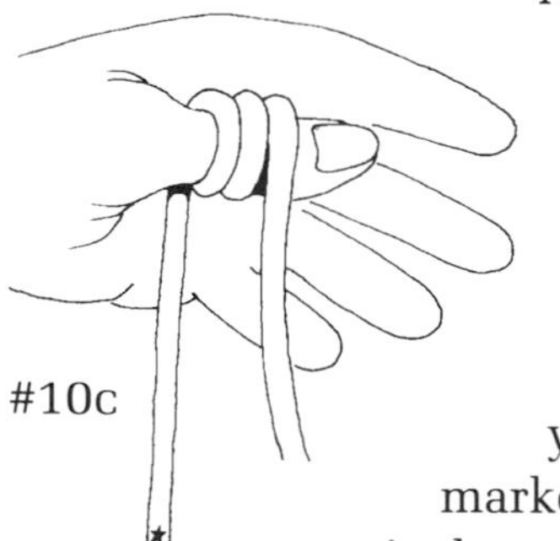

#10c

Tips:

- Begin by demonstrating slowly how you will pass the rope end through the loop (10a). You can point out that your hands are so fast you will release the rope and grasp it again on the other side of the loop without being seen.
- Allow the working end (rope end with the star) to come up from under the thumb, passing between thumb and standing end, as in illustration 10e. Move slowly at first to prevent the thrusted rope from causing a painful jerk to this most essential digit. Chances are you will ignore this caveat, so allow me this, "**I Told You So!**"

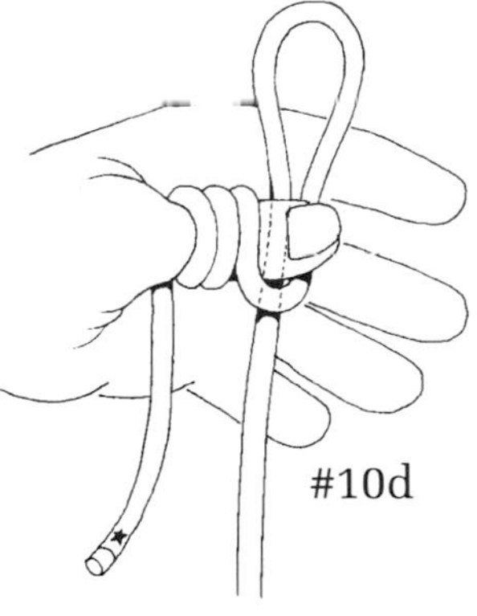

#10d

- Don't start with a working end (starred end) that's too long; 12" is just about right. I won't waste the space explaining what will happen because the result is self-evident, and you're probably going to do it anyway...
- To impress the audience, purposefully fail the first time you make an attempt at *threading the needle*. Purposefully failing is an old magician's ploy that emphasizes the difficulty of what you are trying to do and doubly amazes the troops when you are eventually successful.
- After you have confounded their senses with a successful threading, announce that you will try it just one more time, but that on this final attempt you will reduce the size of the object loop and that (wonder-of-wonders) you will perform the second rapid reeving with YOUR EYES CLOSED. Wow! What more could you do to impress a skeptical group of smiling knotophiles. Don't miss on this final high profile attempt. Persistence is nice; panache is better.

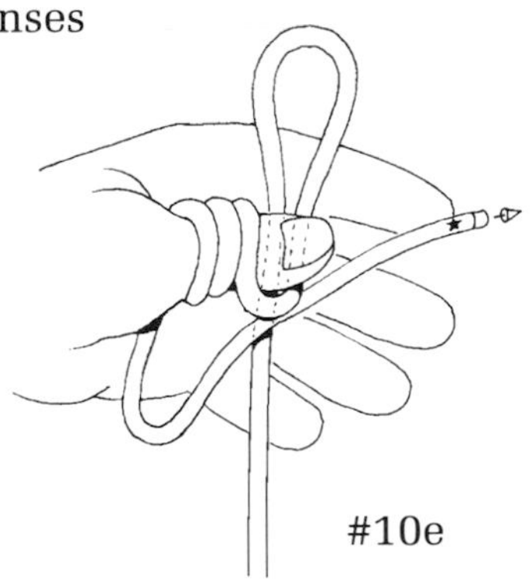

#10e

Puppy Knots a.k.a. Philadelphia Knots

Puppy Knots, when completed, represent a series of evenly-spaced overhand knots tied in a length of rope. Their initial function was to serve as hand-holds in an emergency fire escape rope, but arranging them in sequence as a series of half-

Puppy Knot Sequence

A

B

C

D

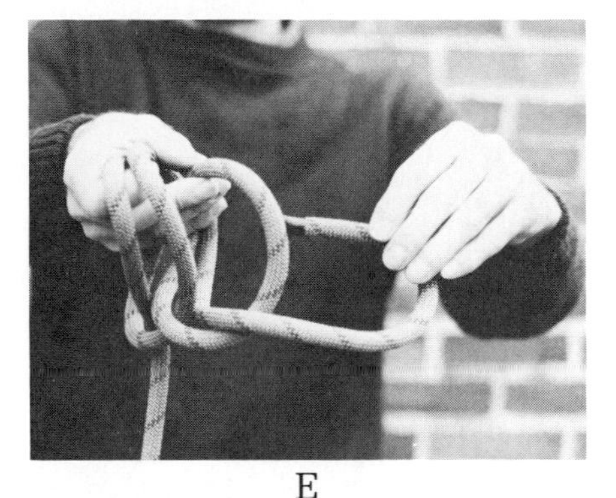
E

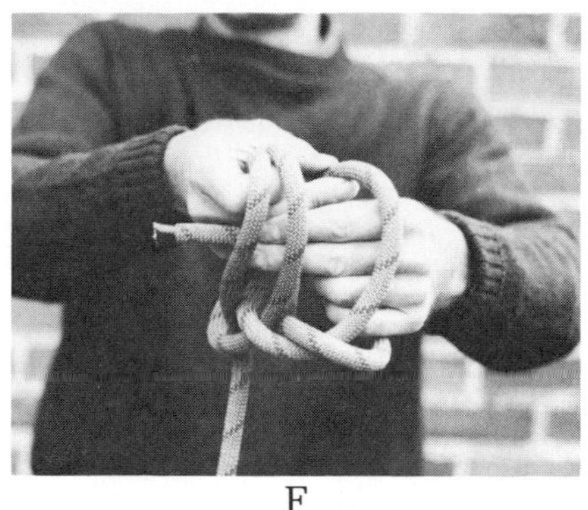
F

G

H

hitches and delighting in their rapid-fire birth-like emergence as reef knots (puppies), provides an undeniable end-in-itself level of satisfaction.

Puppy Knots are for fun; there are no fancy hand movements or intricate moves to memorize. Take a look at the sequenced photos: they represent a series of half-hitches being made in the standing part of the rope, with each half-hitch being laid on top of one another. For each half-hitch made and held, an overhand knot will form itself in the standing part of the rope.

Get someone to hold the end of the working end of the rope, after you have reeved the end through (away from yourself) the overlapping half-hitches. As that person pulls gently, you (as the cordage mid-wife) allow the knots to form and release from the mass of placental rope in your hands. (If all this "let's pretend" parturition fantasy seems inappropriate for your group or yourself, choose another story-line; don't dismiss the knot just because of my weird sense of imagination.)

How many "puppies" can you tie in a 26' long piece of rope? Set regional and state records. The world's record is outasight, so I won't mention it, except to say that I set it — so you better not beat it.

Killick Hitch

This pair of juxtapopsed knots, tied with a piece of nylon cord near the working end of a belay rope, will save you a considerable amount of time and effort as you go about setting up belay systems on your high ropes course.

Many practitioners still set up their high belay ropes by climbing the element supports (trees or poles) and reeving a carried belay rope directly through the carabiners or shear reduction devices that are attached to the belay cable. The benefit of climbing to each SR (Shear Reduction) block is the undeniable exercise received and, more significantly, being able to inspect the belay cable and connecting devices each time the high belay is used. The drawbacks include: too much exercise from having to climb too many supports, being in a hurry and subsequently climbing a tree or pole without a belay, and excess time consumption. There are obviously occasions when you need to climb a tree or pole (safety checking), but on a day-to-day basis, the use of a nylon haul cord that remains permanently attached, makes a lot of time and safety sense.

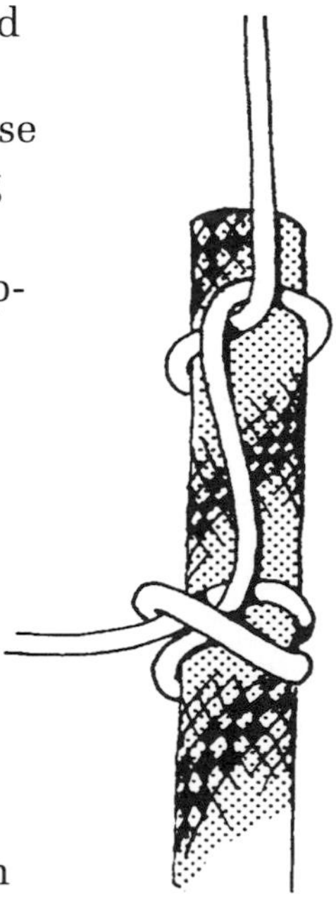

The #4 nylon haul cord (lazy line) can be attached to the end of the belay rope in two ways that have proven successful. The Killick Hitch as illustrated (#11), represents a clove hitch tied with the #4 cord around the climbing rope approximately three inches from the rope's end. A half hitch is added, with the standing part of the cord, about 1/2" from the

#11

rope's end; i.e., as close to the end as possible. This simple knotted arrangement will allow the rope to be pulled through paired locking carabiners or even through the comparatively small orifice of the S/S (spin/static) Pulley. If the cord pulls free of the rope, it means (1) that you didn't tie the Killick Hitch well, and (2) that you get to climb one of the supports to re-establish the belay.

The second haul cord attachment scenario is generally more secure, but requires more initial set-up. The idea is to melt an appropriate sized eye screw into the end of a belay rope, and then attach the nylon haul cord to the eye screw. The beauty of this method is that the pull of the cord is in a direct line with the rope, resulting in easier reeving of the rope through small belay orifices — and you know the potential for embarrassment in that case. The knot of choice in this case is the overhand knot. Reeve the end of the cord through the eye of the screw and tie an overhand knot in the end of the cord (not around the eye screw). That's it, pull away.

Significant Tip — When you reverse the hauling procedure; i.e., when you are taking the belay rope down, retie the lazy line onto the belay rope and **hold onto** the end of that line As gravity accelerates the rope's descent, it may jerk the end of the line from your grasp. Then you get to climb up and check the tightness of the connectors, and take a look at the cable, and ...put the lazy line back through the SR device.

When you initially cut the #4 cord to size, both ends of the severed line will cowstail, no matter how sharp your edge. Trying to coax a fluffy nylon end through a small eye screw opening can be camel-frustrating, and a huge waste of time.

Do this. Put a glove (not a dress glove) on your left hand. Fire up a butane torch (a cigarette lighter will do, and in a pinch, even a match works OK), and touch the flame to the #4 cowstail, turning it into a blob of melted and evil-smelling poly material. If the cord end catches on fire and continues to burn, you touched it too much.

Let the blob cool for a few seconds and then gently roll the malleable half-melted plastic between your thumb and forefinger: right... use the gloved hand. This gently rolling action shapes the cooling end of the cord into a hardened point, which you'll find much easier to reeve through the screw eye than a fluffy cowstail. Just another little cordage trick to make the job easier; and add to your image.

If you already know how to melt an eye screw into the rope, skip these next couple paragraphs. (I just thought to myself, "How many people would possibly know or care to know, how to melt an eye screw into the end of a rope?" Right,...so I guess you're still here.) Hold the eye screw on the eye end with a pair

Eye Screw Sequence

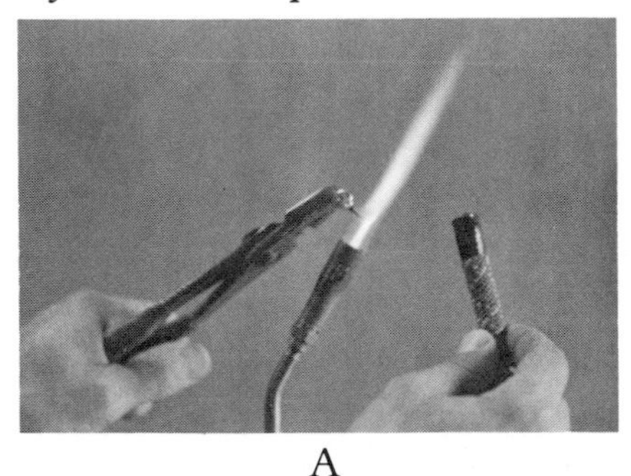

A

B

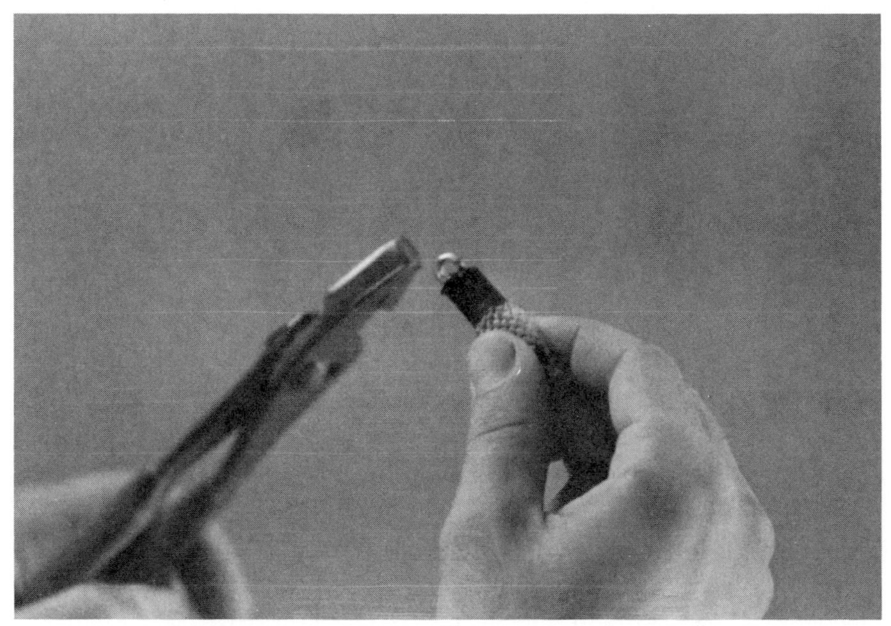

C

of pliers or vise grips. Heat up the screw end with a butane torch until the threads glow red (takes about ten seconds). Insert the hot screw end into the heat-sealed end of the belay rope until the base of the eye rests directly against the glassy end of the rope (See Eye Screw Sequence.) Shoving a red hot piece of metal into most nylon substances is going to produce acrid smoke, so don't breathe the fumes. It's best to perform this tricky maneuver outdoors. **Caveat** — If the end of the eye screw is indeed RED hot, let it cool just a bit, otherwise it will literally melt a small pool of nylon in the rope end and float out when you let go with the pliers. It's interesting to watch, so go ahead and try it.

Prusik Knot

This is one of the only knots that was named after an individual, in this case the man who developed the knot, Dr. Carl Prusik. People think of this knot as somewhat esoteric, coming into use only during those rare situations when a rescue is being carried out, but the practical applications are many including ropes course construction, tying down a canoe on the roof of a car, tightening tent guy ropes, etc.

The illustrations (#12a–c) preclude my having to tell you how to tie the knot, but here's a couple tips about using the Prusik.

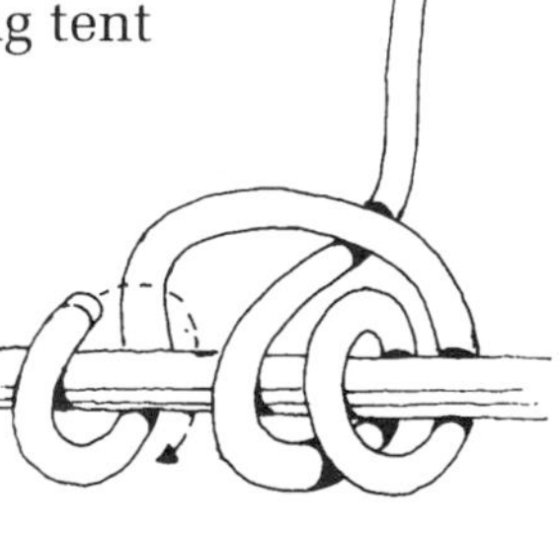

#12a

After you tie the knot, *dress it up.* That's knot-talk for making sure all the rope strands that make up the knot are symmetrically arranged and not binding on one another. Any knot will only function to its maximum potential if *dressed* properly.

When using the Prusik knot for ascending or descending a vertical rope, don't put your hand on the knot itself, as the downward hand pressure that you inadvertently apply might just be enough to loosen the knot's friction hold, and cause both you and the knot to descend

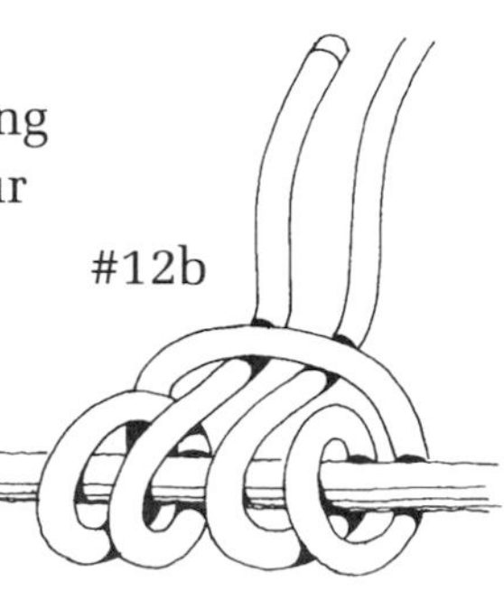

#12b

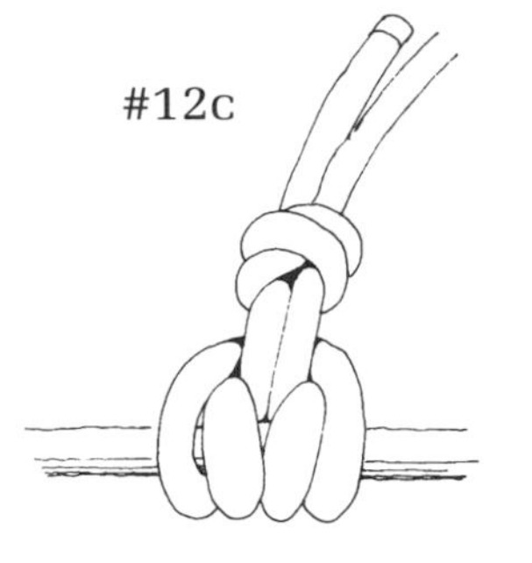

rapidly — as per the inexorable and wholly predictable laws of gravity.

If a heavy load is applied to the knot, it may be necessary for you to loosen the knot's grip on the standing part of the rope before it will slide in either direction.

A better grip is achieved if the standing rope is of a greater diameter than the rope used for tying the Prusik knot. (Ref. James Bond movie sequence where Bond prusiks up a long section of climbing rope using his Kevlar shoe laces. Too much!)

Butterfly Knot

I was planning initially not to include this knot, because a bowline on-a-bight can be substituted nicely, but thinking back to the many knot-tying sessions I've lead over the years, the Butterfly knot used to be a favorite. So, making a big comeback, heeeeere's *THE BUTTERFLY KNOT.*

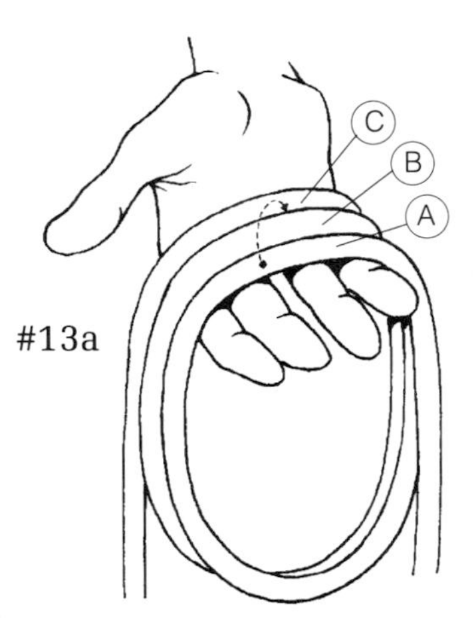

This whimsically-named knot is best used when you need a non-tightening loop in the middle of the rope. If dressed properly it will not jam under pressure and the formed loop will not slip. An additional plus is that the tying sequence is visually appealing and makes you look good, as hands and fingers fly through the coils and turns that make up the knot. Ready to look good? Here's how.

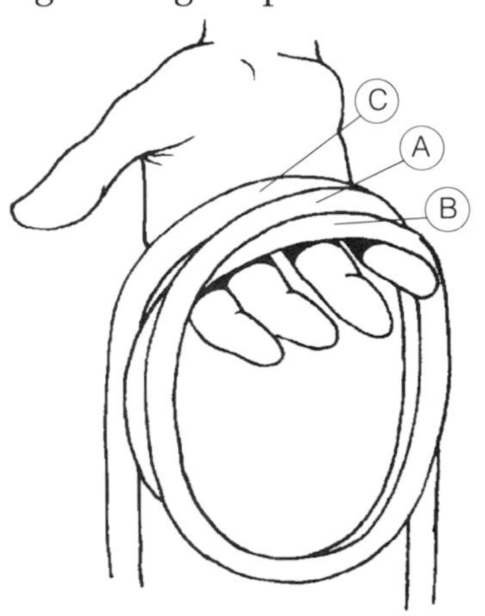

#13b

Place that portion of the rope bight where you want the

knot to be tied, in the palm of your right hand. As you hold your palm directly in front of your body, the rope should run across your palm, between your thumb and index finger, and across the meaty karate part of your hand. Grasp that part of the rope that is the closest to your body with your left hand, and swing a 6"–8" diameter loop below your right hand, placing the working end of the loop in your palm next to the rope section already there. Make sure that second section of rope rests to the finger side of the strand already in your palm; not toward your wrist. Do exactly the same thing again so that you have two equal loops below your hand and three side-by-side strands in your palm (#13a).

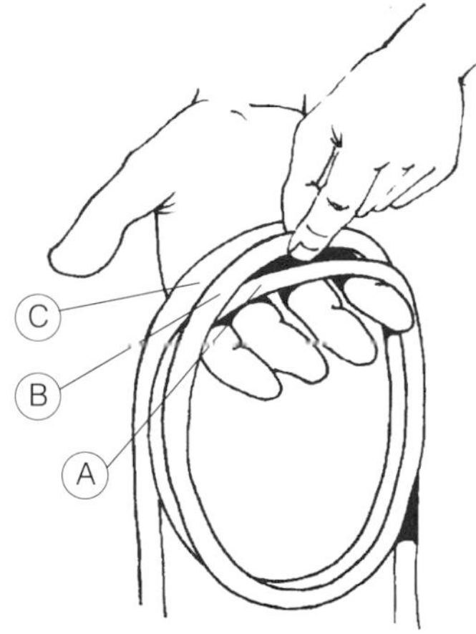

#13c

#13d

Using the index finger and thumb of your left hand, lift strand **A** and place it between strands **B & C** on your palm (#13b). Again, using your left hand, pinch strand **B** and move it over the tops of strands **A & C** (#13c) so that strand **B** rests on the palm of your right hand (#13d). Starting near the right finger tips, slide the fingers of your left hand under strands **A & C** on your palm and grab the third strand, **B**. Pull strand **B** toward the

#13e

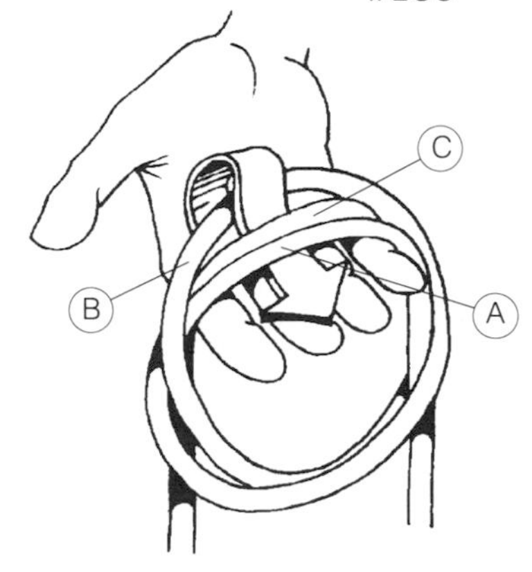

fingertips, under the two remaining palm strands (#13e). As you continue to pull that third strand, the entire configuration will come off your right hand. Continue to pull strand **B** with the left hand, and move your right hand to grasp the two standing ends; slowly pull your hands apart. The forming knot now should look like #13f, but don't spend too much time admiring the resemblance, because we're not done yet.

#13f

To finish the sequence (great image move coming up), with a rope end in each hand, pull abruptly and simultaneously in opposite directions.

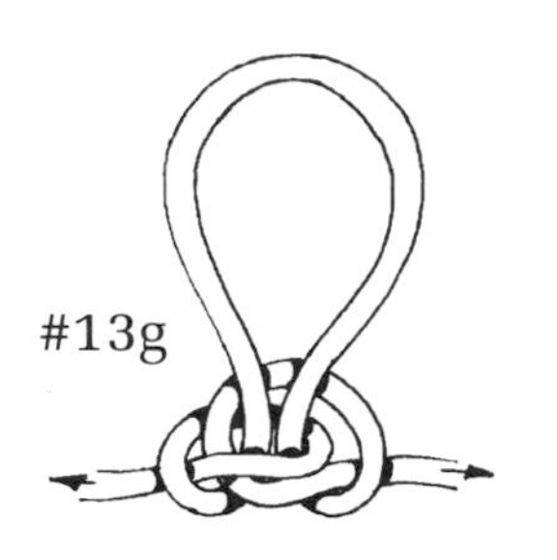
#13g

This flamboyantly confident move will change an amorphous mass of nascent looped rope into an ephemeral arrangement of butterfly-like strands and threads that float in lambent images from carabiner to staple. Rhetorically measured at 99.5% on the BS scale; not quite pure, but there's your knot and useable loop anyway (#13g).

Timber Hitch

This easily-tied hitch is not useful for tying in a belay or setting up a rappel, but for hauling logs and timbers, it's a winner. The tying sequence is so easy, and as a finished hitch looks so loose, that you may at first dismiss its holding power and usefulness. The finished Timber Hitch provides a good visual and kinetic lesson in the holding power of friction.

Take a turn of rope around the plank or log to be lifted at just about the balance point of that object. Wrap the working end of the rope back onto itself so that at least three tucks or wraps are made (#14a). It has been indicated to me that the wraps should always follow the lay of the rope (if you are using laid rope), but on occasion I have been in a hurry and have wrapped against the lay of the rope with

#14a

equally good results. What you have just tied is a Timber Hitch, and by itself won't hold or function well as a pulling anchor hitch. To complete an efficient hauling combination, take the standing part of the rope as it comes off the Timber Hitch and tie a half hitch near the end of the plank or pole. The half hitch orients the pull of the rope in the desired direction (up or horizontal), while the Timber Hitch provides the frictioned holding power of the hitch combination.(#14b)

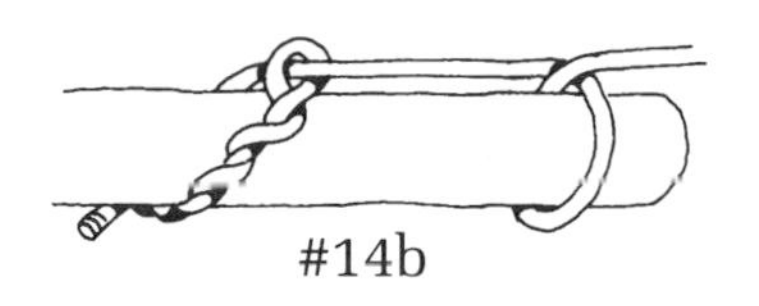
#14b

The cartoon illustration (#14c) shows a determined fellow attempting to pull a log somewhere. His hitches are well done, but the straight pull that he is applying won't get him anywhere because the end of the log is digging into the ground. Avoid his frustration by slightly elevating the half hitch end of the log.

#14c

When tension is released from the rope, both the half hitch and the Timber Hitch will release easily without jamming. Great stuff, eh? This is one of those slightly esoteric combinations that make you look like you know what you're doing. Use it!

Eye and End Splicing

"The sailmaker opens his strands with a wooden fid. When his splice is complete he pounds it with his fid and often spits on the handle and burnishes the splice to make it lie fair..."

Ashley

Now I'm going to introduce you to simplistic splicing, because it's about time you learned, and splicing is something you should want to know anyway, being a professional adventurer, and all...

Why splice? Isn't knotting easier and don't knots allow greater flexibility? Yes, and yes, that's why knot books get written, but splicing provides a considerably stronger and more aesthetic method of not only joining two ropes, but also forming a permanent eye in the end of three-strand rope. Certain braided ropes can be spliced, but the technique is beyond me, and doesn't apply to ropes course use, so let's stick with something attainable and useful. But wait..., if spicing is so great, why not use a splice instead of a knot all the time? Excellent question. Did you take this course before? Specifically: splicing takes considerably longer than tying a knot, and undoing the splice is even less convenient (inconceivable) when you want to move the rope for additional use.

Plynn really gets to show his stuff now. Splicing three-strand rope isn't hard, just initially confusing, and I think much of that confusion results from trying to learn splicing from a book (text and illustrations), rather than having someone knowledgeable at your elbow to indicate why the illustration is so confoundedly complex when the manipulation is so basically simple.

Plynn has a way of visually separating the strands so that you can SEE what is happening step-by-step, as evidenced by his clear knot illustrations. Refer to the text in a pinch, but the illustrations are where-it's-at when it comes to splicing.

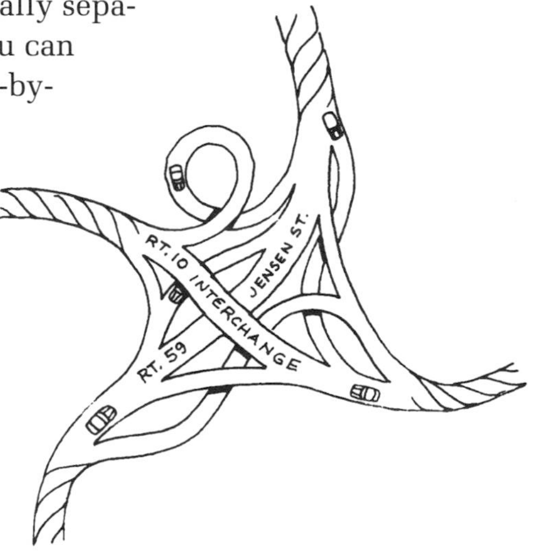

We will be working on the eye splice only, because the short splice (connecting two lengths of rope together) is seldom used in a ropes course context. I can't remember the last time I used a short splice... Since you're about to learn the eye splice, and the splicing manipulations are practically identical, let's save the short splice for another time. How about I show you during the next PA workshop? Good, it's a deal. You'll have to remind me tho'.

Eye Splice

Let's splice! After cutting the rope, unlay the rope about 10 inches and tape the ends of the three strands (A, B, and C) separately with black electrician's tape — if you have only red or blue tape, that's fine too. If you don't tape the strand ends during this learning process, you will eventually end up with three world-class cowstails.

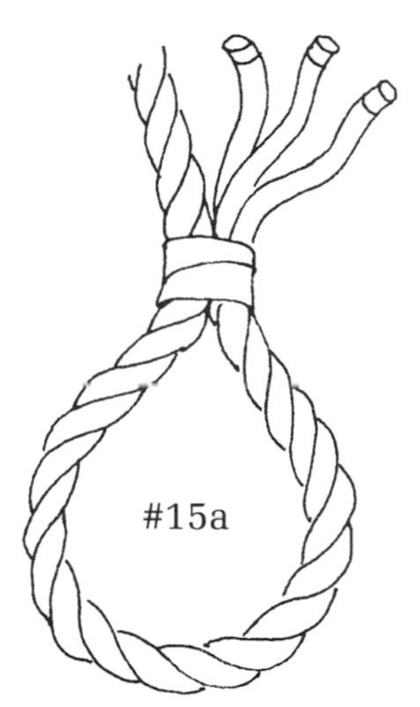

For the sake of clarity, only the first drawing of this sequence (#15a) shows the taping process that temporarily secures the working end of the rope to the standing part; i.e., the area where the strands that you are splicing join the bight of rope. (The two little arrows on illustration #15c indicate where the rope would be taped back to itself.) Splicing can be accomplished without this taping, but while you're learning, joining the rope sections together with tape makes the process a whole lot easier.

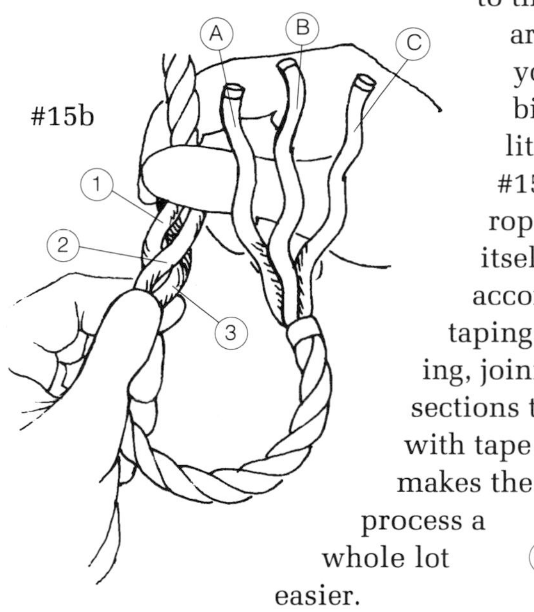

Illustrations #15c–f indicate the first three tucks necessary to make a *grand-tuck*. These three movements involve the insertion of the working strand ends **A**, **B**, and **C** into the lay of the rope in positions **1**, **2**, and **3**.

You will be inserting the **A-B-C**

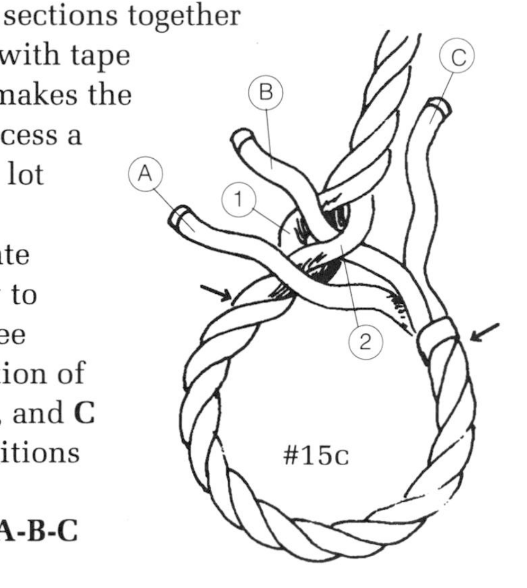

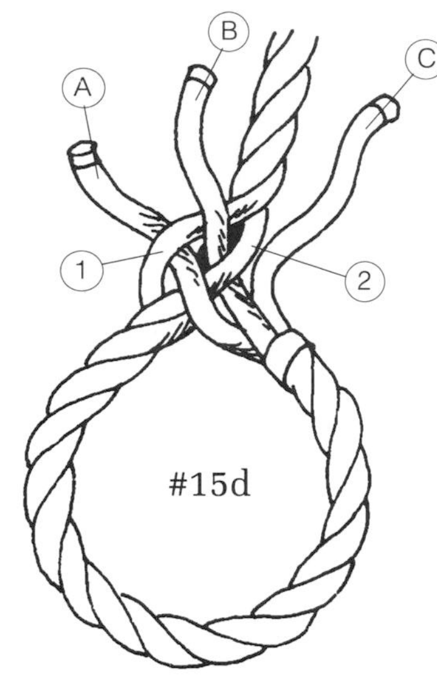

#15d

working strands back into the **1-2-3** standing strands of the rope (#15b). Begin by taking working strand **B** (it's the middle strand), and insert (tuck) it into the lay of the rope (#15c). Wherever you do this determines standing strand **2**. Then take working strand **A** and insert it into the standing lay of the rope one strand to the left of strand **2**. (Keep looking at the illustrations, #15d in this case) The strand you just went under becomes standing strand **1**. That leaves you with working strand **C** to be put under standing strand **3**. If you can't find or decide where this is supposed to happen, turn the entire eye splice operation over (#15e) and you should find the unused (no one has stuck anything under it yet) standing strand **3**: stick working strand **C** under it. (#15f).

#15e

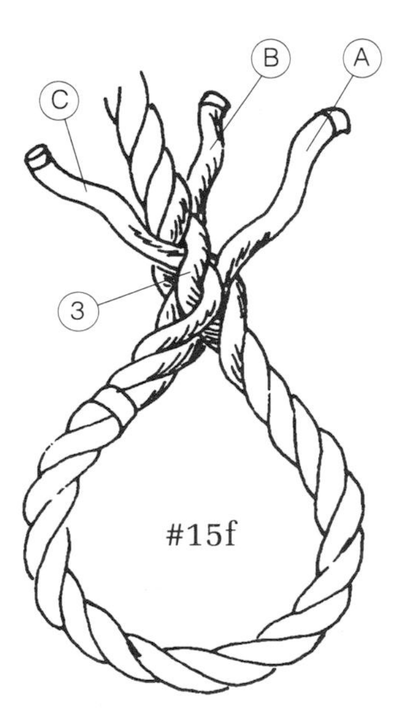

#15f

If you did these three tucks correctly, you have made a *grand-tuck.* If correct, the three working strands should all exit the standing rope at the same level and in three different directions. Congratulations, those first three tucks are the hardest part of splicing.

Now begin the **A-B-C** into **1-2-3**

insertion process again. Start with any one of the working strands (illustration #15g indicates starting with **B**), and begin an over and under insertion (tucking) process; i.e., the working strand must go over the standing strand that is next in line (it's actually leaning on it; touching it) and then under the next standing strand. Do the same thing with **A** and **C**, remembering that you may have to turn the operation over to find out where **C** should be inserted. This completes the second grand-tuck. In natural fiber rope (manila, sisal), three grand-tucks (9 separate insertions) provide maximum strength. Five grand-tucks are necessary to reach the same tensile level in synthetic laid rope (multiline).

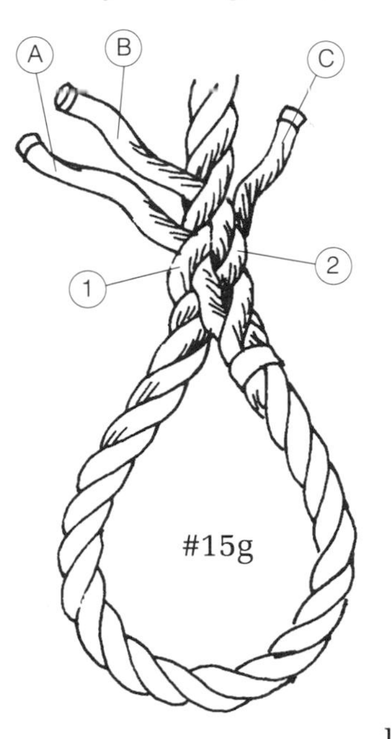

After you have fashioned the proper number of grand-tucks, cut off the remaining **A-B-C** ends, so that at least 1/2" of rope remains to fray (cowstail). This bit of fray/fluff keeps the three strand ends of the rope from pulling back into the standing rope. Do not burn (melt) the frayed ends, because of the probability of melting a portion of the standing rope — remember that nylon melts very easily.

If you want to include a thimble in the eye of your splice, the placing of the thimble must be done at the beginning of the splicing process. Bend the rope around the thimble and tape the base of the working ends to the standing part of the rope; i.e., wrap the tape around the ropes at the bottom of the tear-shaped thimble. Apply the tape firmly so that this juncture remains solid during the manipulation of the first tuck. As you make the first three **A-B-C** tucks, pull them up snugly to the base of the thimble (the taped area). Remove the tape when you have finished the splice. I guess there's nothing wrong with leaving the plastic wrap there, but it looks neater and more organic if you remove it.

Hey, there's your splice. Nice going! If it looks a little rough, put the splice under your foot on the floor and applying some pressure, briskly roll the splice back and forth underfoot. Looks better, eh? Just an old seaman's trick that makes you look like you know what you're doing. *"An ounce of image is worth a pound of performance."*

End or Back Splice

Initially, this end-of-the-rope splice seems to have only a cosmetic function, but there's more to it than looks alone. Back splicing takes the place of whipping or having to use copious amounts of tape to finish off a cut end of rope. Also, the increased diameter that results from end splicing provides a more substantial area to grip the rope end. Sybaritically considered, needing to perform 10–15 back splices is a grand excuse to spend extended periods sitting in the sun.

#16a

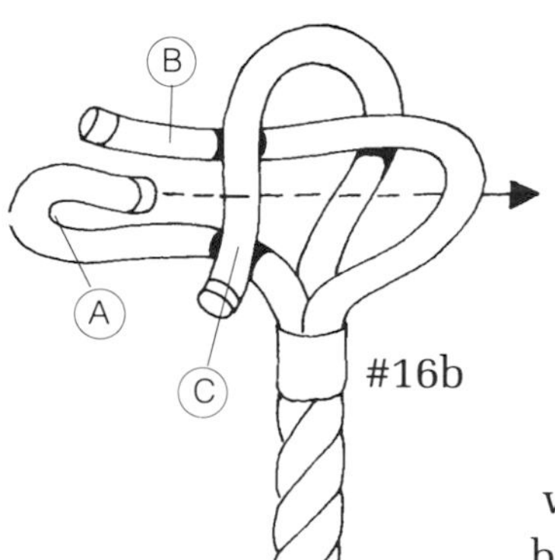

#16b

Plynn's illustration of the start, (forming the crown knot) can't be enhanced by my writing, so just unlay your rope, tape the three ends to prevent unraveling, and follow the sequential diagrams. Those of you who have back spliced in the past may be confused by the drawings, because there is more than one way to arrive at a crown knot. If you know another way to arrive at the same destination, stick with it.

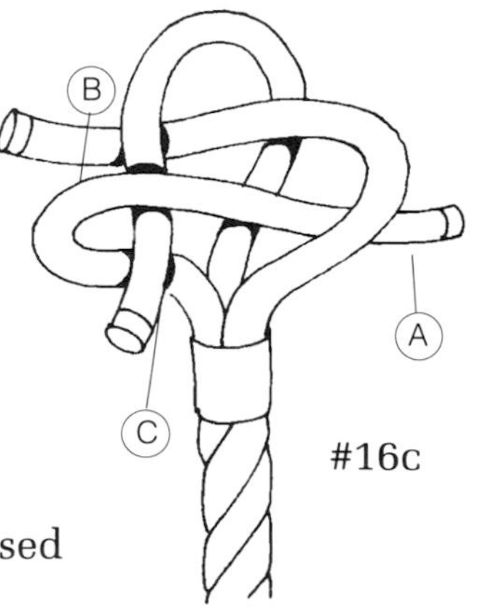

#16c

Once the crown knot is tied and dressed

(as you dress up the knot, pull each strand in sequence, then move to the next one until you have applied equal tension to every strand and the crown looks tight and symmetrical when viewed on end) treat the three strand ends as if you had just finished the first grand-tuck while eye splicing. Ends, **A**, **B**, and **C**, are to be interwoven back into the standing part of the rope under strands **1**, **2**, and **3**, using the over and under technique. Refer to the eye splice illustrations in the previous section.

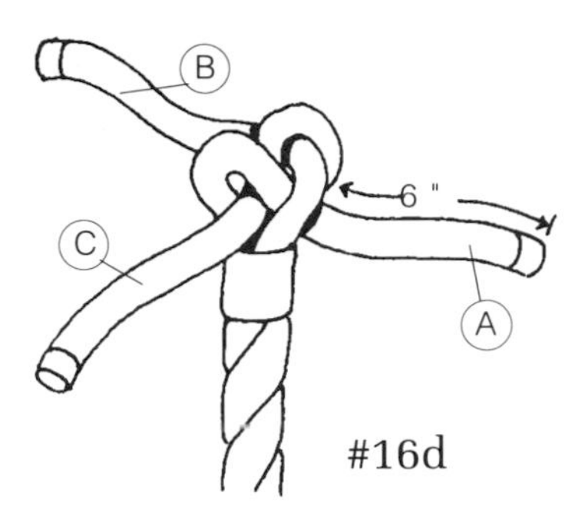

#16d

After taking 4–5 grand-tucks, roll that sucker under foot, then admire the best looking back splice that you ever made.

#16e

Special Techniques and Applications

Zip Wire and Fidget Ladder Tightening Process

I discovered two things while building ropes courses (...actually a few more than two, but two will do for now), that will save you much planning time and considerable effort.

I used to build indoor zip wires utilizing a turnbuckle to tighten the cable, which also allowed a convenient put-up/take-down capability. I don't do that anymore.

I used to attach a fidget ladder directly between two supports, clipping in each end. I don't do that anymore either. Here's why:

The maximum take-up on a 5/8" turnbuckle is only 12"; i.e., I had 12" to play with (plan with) as I determined where I should cut the cable: I had to measure and cut carefully; a predictably anxiety-ridden construction juncture that I now neatly avoid. Also, putting on and taking off a turnbuckle (or lots of them) isn't much fun unless you are trying to develop Popeye forearms.

If you attach a fidget ladder directly from tree to tree with carabiners, the measurement between trees has to be just-so, or it's a no-fit situation. Then when you do find just the right trees, the multiline rope begins to stretch and the ladder ends up scraping the ground before you know it.

I don't want to change your building style or get into ropes course construction at all, but the simple use of a rope, and a couple carabiners (or rapid links) and knowledge of the mechanical advantage inherent in pulley sustems, I think will convince you that this simple tightening technique has merit.

If your fidget ladder is 18' long, find two supports that are about 20' apart. Clip one end of your fidget to the high support staple. (I am assuming that you know how to place a staple, attach a fidget ladder, etc. If not, you may be interested in another of Project Adventure's how-to books, *Challenge by Choice,* that details how to build a low ropes course. If this section you're reading now has no practical application for you, don't continue reading it — I wouldn't.)

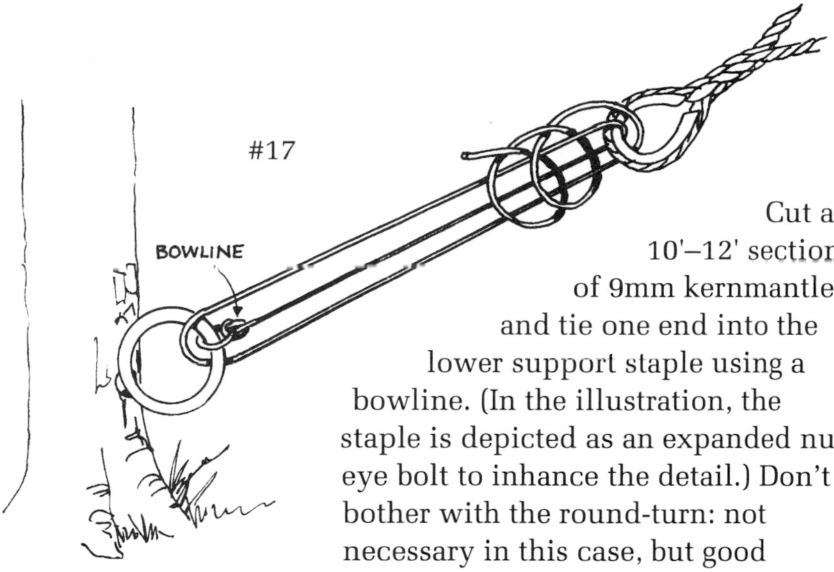

#17

BOWLINE

Cut a 10'–12' section of 9mm kernmantle and tie one end into the lower support staple using a bowline. (In the illustration, the staple is depicted as an expanded nut eye bolt to inhance the detail.) Don't bother with the round-turn: not necessary in this case, but good thinking nonetheless. Reeve the working end of the rope through the metal thimble at the unclipped lower end of the fidget ladder. Bring that working end toward the tree support and reeve it through the lower staple; correct, the staple (expanded eye bolt) to which you tied the initial bowline. Bring it back and reeve it again through the thimble and pull hard on what's left of the working end until the fidget ladder is at the tightness you desire. Finish off with a couple half hitches tied around all the rope strands and near the thimble. Tie as many half hitches as you like, but two will do it (#17).

See what I mean; you have an easily adjusted fidget ladder that is perfectly secure. No worries.

The zip wire attachment and tightening scenario follows about the same procedure, but I don't want to detail those steps because offering construction information is beyond the scope of this book. If you are really interested, give me or Project Adventure a call, and we'll talk about it.

Rollo's Wrap — A Self-Belay

A bottom belay set-up (sling-shot type belay from the ground) provides constant and comforting protection, but the belayer, attentive to your every move, is a worker that could be doing something else productive while you're steadfastly

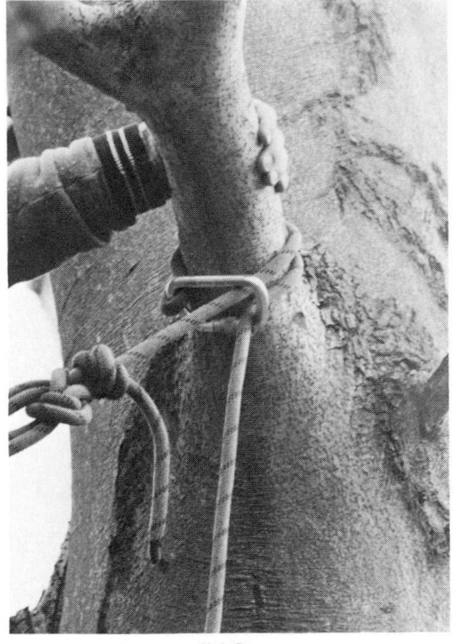

#18a

thrashing about in the trees. Consider using the following simple and effective static self-belay technique: Rollo's Wrap.

Rollo Sapsucker was, and undoubtedly still is, a most inept climber. Using his name (Rollo Sapsucker is a fictitious name, but close enough to maintain the profound attention to detail so inimical to the text of this tome) for this efficient belay set-up seems appropriate considering Rollo's propensity for *falling* — a panicked exclamation heard with some frequency whenever his splayed and quivering body made it more than eight feet off the ground. The next time you are working at height and your belayer could obviously be doing something else productive, situate yourself solidly amidst the tree canopy and ask for some slack in the belay rope. Arrange a large loop in the slack belay rope and pass that formed loop around the **base** of a convenient and substantial limb. The base of this branch should be located slightly above you (#18a). (Notice that I am allowing considerable judgmental leeway as to positioning and limb size: be conservative, recognizing that some tree limbs are much stronger than others. If in doubt, include the tree trunk as part of the limb wrap.) As the loop passes around the limb, clip a locking

#18b

carabiner through the loop and also include the standing part (rope leading to the belayer) and working end (rope leading to you) in the carabiner (18b). Lock the carabiner gate and pull the loop snugly to the limb. Yell "*Off Belay,*" or "*Belay Off*" (depending on which climbing school you attended), to your rope handler and relax as you enjoy this tree-top tie-in, and watch your grounded counterpart now take up the more mundane and often less appealing tasks of ropes course construction (bark stripping, post hole digging, brush clearing, etc.) Rollo's Wrap can be adjusted for length if you need more or less rope for whatever working position you find yourself in.

Using a carabiner in this way loads the minor axis against the tree limb, a safety no-no in most circumstances, however this set up, utilizing a short section of static rope, would not receive a high shock load. Don't give yourself more slack rope than is absolutely necessary to complete your construction task; even a short fall on a static rope can be ____________. (Fill in an appropriate cruncher word to remind yourself of the negative consequences.)

Studebaker and Swiss Seat Pelvic Wraps

Pay close attention now, this one's a biggie. You will probably be using the following tying sequences over and over during high time on the ropes course — unless you decide to use harnesses. If you have decided to use a commercial harness for student use, skip this highly entertaining and informative section and move your play piece immediately to **Harnesses**. See you soon...

Swiss seats (SS) and Studebaker Wraps (SW) are self-tied pelvic support systems that provide a *fairly* comfortable anatomical connecting point for the belay rope; as contrasts the single bowline around the waist, which is *fairly* uncomfortable. The material for either seat or wrap can be rope (9 mm kernmantle) or webbing (1" tubular). The rope is somewhat stronger, but the webbing is more comfortable: take your pick. The wild colors available in either rope or webbing will allow you to make whatever fashion statement seems most appropriate for your climbing mood, or sartorial ascent ensemble.

Project Adventure recommends a length of 18' for tying a SS

(rope or webbing) and 26' for the SW. These lengths are for the normal adult. If your clientele is not normal (elementary age, or well-covered) experiment with various lengths so that you don't end up with lots of wrap left over, wondering where to tuck or stick the excess. Be aware that kernmantle rope will shrink over a period of time, particularly after being soaked. Better cut 19' and 27' in anticipation of this length reduction.

Whatever group you are working with, there is bound to be an individual that is "well covered" to the extreme. That person is usually reluctant to tie in anyway, and the fact that none of the lengths are long enough for their ample bods, tips the participation scale to, "I'll sit this one out." Cut a few extra long sling lengths and mark them unobtrusively so that you can hand a longer length to that person who needs it without drawing attention to his/her need. DON'T cut all hot pink lengths for the full-figure group; you might as well write **CHUBBY** on their foreheads.

The SS is easier to tie and doesn't take as long to learn, but has a tendency to loosen and slip down on the thighs while climbing. If you are clipping in people for a series of simple climbs that don't require long-term wearing of the wrap, the SS is a functional and prudent choice.

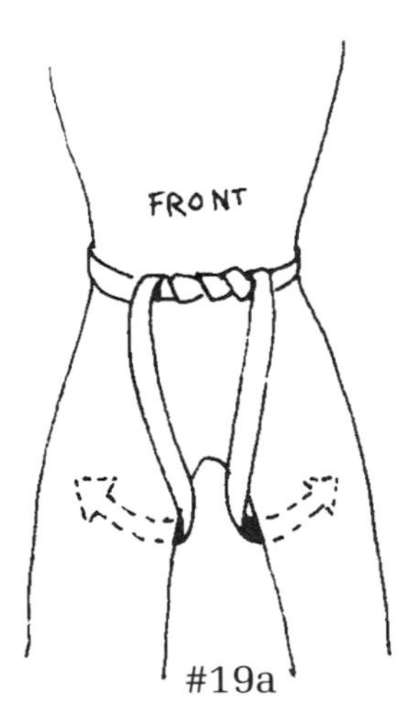

#19a

The SW takes longer to learn and requires a longer length of tying material. Once tied, however, this wrap provides somewhat more support and will not easily slide down from the pelvic position. The SW is a particularly good choice if you are clipping the student in from behind (trapeze jump).

Whichever self-tied pelvic support system you choose, be aware that after experiencing a fall or controlled lowering, it's a good idea to retie either seat type. Slack *will* develop in the strands and wraps as the result of the gravity and/or falling forces applied.

OK, here we go. Grab your section of rope or webbing and find the center. Place that center point on your right hip (left hip for left-handers) at about the belly button level, and hold it there. Feel for the hip bone and make sure this initial wrap stays above that point. If you can't feel the ilial crest of the pelvis (or you don't want to), line up the wrap with your navel. Holding the center point on your hip, reach around behind with your free hand and bring that half of the wrap up to your navel. Slide your right hand forward to meet the left hand. After doing this you should have a single wrap around your waist, but most significantly at this juncture, the working ends should be of *unequal* length, differing by about 12–18 inches. Check and see if you are interested, but if you handled the webbing as instructed, the ends will be *just right.* (Ref. The Goldilock's rule)

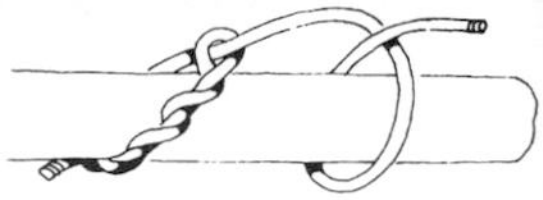

Tie an overhand knot at your belly button. If you want this first tie to remain secure, as you continue the tying sequence, take another turn beyond the simple overhand to fashion a surgeon's knot. It only takes a few more seconds and not much wrap, so you might as well do it.

Take both working ends (the only two ends you have) and pass them both down between your legs, making **SURE** that the wraps remain separated; i.e., don't cross them in the groin area. (Gentlemen, beware!) Reach behind, separate the two lengths, and bring them forward, separately on each side of the hips. Are you checking the illustrations?

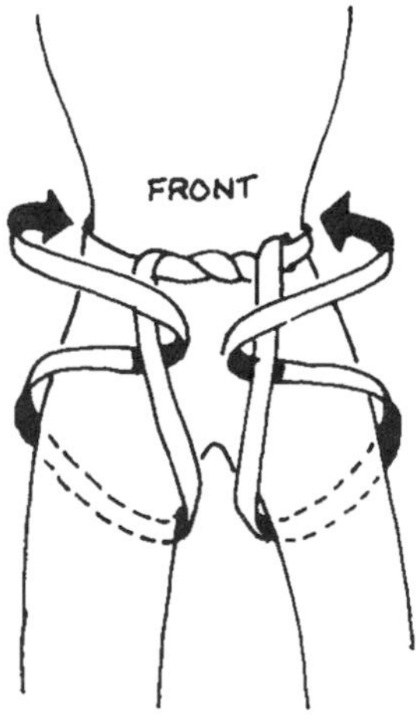

FRONT

#19b

Take the two ends, and individually put them under the two vertical sections of wrap that go down between your legs — front to back or back to front — it doesn't make enough difference to worry about. Pull the two reeved ends out and away from the body to keep the wrap tight. Pass both ends behind the body, crossing them at about the small of the back, and continue around the body in either direction until the lengths meet on the left hip (opposite the hip you started on). If everything has gone well, the working ends should be of equal length, and if your body size is median-mode there should now be just enough to tie a finishing square knot with two safety knots — one double overhand (tunnel) knot on either side of the square knot. What you have just fashioned is a *Swiss Seat* (#19b). The connecting carabiner is clipped in through all the rope or webbing material located at the navel area. (If you don't clip through ALL the wrap material at this juncture, the Swiss Seat becomes a Swiss Squeezer. You won't die, but it's uncomfortable... no, it's more than that; it hurts, don't do it.)

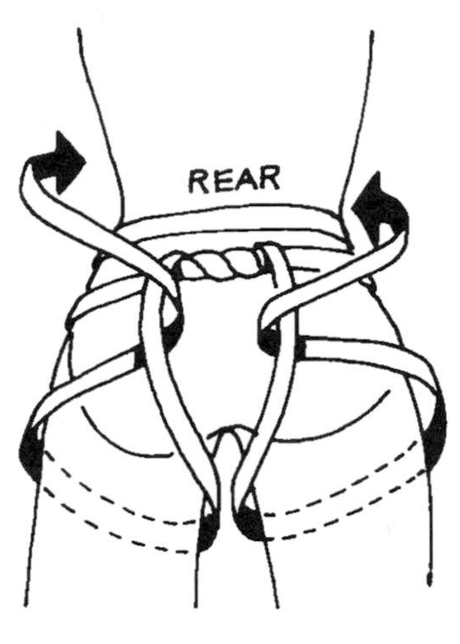

#19c

Also notice that the finishing knot is tied *off to the side* so that there can be no confusion as to where to clip the carabiner — right in front, with no knots in the way to confuse the novice.

Someone is bound to take umbrage (that means, be respectfully horrified) with your (my) choice of a finishing knot As I explained earlier, a square knot isn't the greatest, but considering the circumstance, it's the best for our use. I said all that to say this: tie whatever you want as a finishing knot as long as there are back up safety knots on each side of the securing knot.

Let's backtrack a bit so that we can get on with the *Studebaker Wrap* (#19c). The SW is essentially a double SS, tied front and back. So there we were, with both rope/webbing ends in hand after having reeved the ends through the groin wraps. Take those ends, and rather than tying a finishing knot (SS), take the strands and tie an overhand knot right at the small of your back. (Take an additional wrap around if you want the surgeon's knot holding ability — optional tho'.)

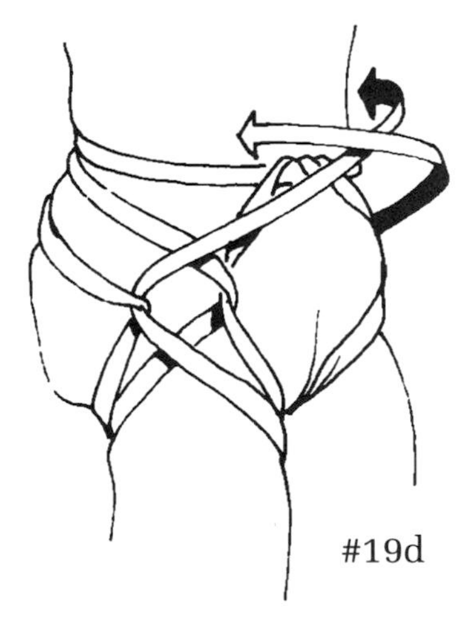
#19d

Pass both strands down between your legs again, this time from back to front. Same warning as before; don't cross the strands in the groin area. Separate the strands and pass them from front to back across the hips (#19d). (Remember, you are duplicating the movements that you made while tying the SS, except on the dorsal part of your bod.) Pass the working ends under and through the wraps that run somewhat vertically down and across your gluteus maximus (your ever-loving cheeks)... disappearing into the nether land of wedgies. As before, reeve the rope ends front to back or back to front — doesn't matter much.

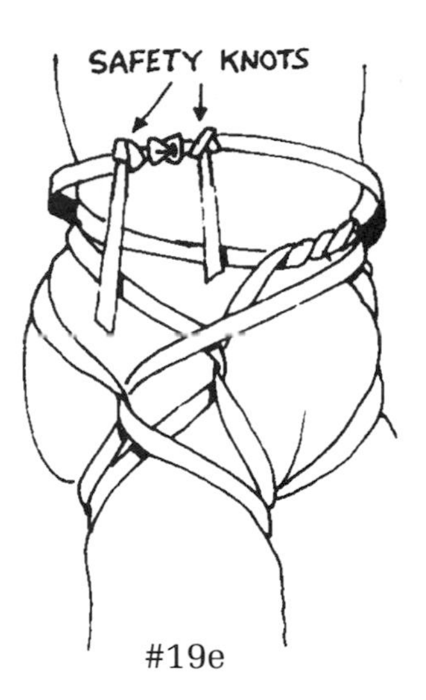

#19e

Bring the ends to the front across the hips again, and depending upon how much rope or webbing you have left, wrap the ends around your waist until you end up with enough wrap left to tie a finishing square knot with safeties (#19e). That's the *Studebaker Wrap,* so called because your encumbered pelvis faintly resembles a 1952 Studebaker automobile. Remember (those of you over 40) the '52 Studebaker looked the same coming and going. Get it? Look in the mirror. Turn around.

#19f

Check out the cartoon (#19f). Still don't get it? Sorry, you're too young.

You should, at this terminal wrapping juncture, feel pelvically bonded, but safe. It should be more obvious now that you can either clip in front or back and get the same belay support. The dorsal clip-in, utilizing two locking carabiners, makes diving for a Pamper Pole trapeze more comfortable and plausible. No? Come on... this is the Wide Wonderful World of Adventure; get psyched.

Harnesses

Didn't take you long to get here, but then I know where you're coming from. Don't tell me... you don't have enough class time for tying the wraps, right? I can appreciate the quandary; you want the students to be responsible for their own safety system, but you don't have the time or assistance personnel to teach a self-tied arrangement — the Swiss Seat or Studebaker Wrap. So let's take a look at what else is available and some of the pros and cons of wraps vs. the harness.

There are lots of harnesses on the market, from an industrial full-body arrangement to the lightweight variety that rock climbers use, and considering that all of them must meet certain industry standards, it's hard to go wrong from a safety standpoint. Some are more substantially made than others and will therefore last longer, but generally, any harness that is sold commercially and has an established trade name will provide both comfort and safety. If you buy something from a friend who has recently purchased an industrial grade sewing machine, and has an idea for a harness that will "revolutionize the market," you deserve the results. Be creatively commercial with your purchase of curriculum game materials, not with safety gear.

Be aware that harness manufacturers are very cognizant of product liability laws, and therefore will not be understanding of your request to use the harness in such a way as to revoke the carefully worded and inclusive guarantee. For example, most harnesses are manufactured for ventral (front) attachment only. Your intention to use a dorsal (back) clip-in will not be well received, and will not be included in the manufacturer's guarantee.

The obvious benefit of using a harness is ease of use with the resultant saving of time, a valuable commodity in a 47-minute class. Another benefit is the comfort factor: a commercial harness is definitely (sometimes marginally) more comfortable than a self-tied seat.

Drawbacks of buying a commercially made harness include cost (a decent harness will run $30.00–$80.00, as compared to about $6.50 for the tubular webbing needed to tie a Studebaker Wrap), and *things* that can go wrong. *Things* such as not rereeving the securing strap back through the buckle, clipping into auxiliary nylon loops that have nothing to do with securing the harness, and putting on the harness incorrectly.

No attempt is made in this book to provide instruction in harness fitting or use, as each manufacturer should provide specific information about the use of their safety product. If they do not, I'd suggest not buying that particular harness.

Coiling a Rope

Ropes course truism: "If you don't teach your students early-on how to coil rope, **you** will have much rope to coil." True enough; so after you learn one of these coiling techniques, teach it quickly to someone else — kind of a hands-on hot potato.

The Hangman's or Alpine Coil

If you know how to tie a hangman's knot, this coiling technique will seem familiar; but then doesn't everyone know how to tie this macabre knot? (How did you get through summer school algebra classes without positioning your chair next to a window that had a too-long sash cord within reach; perfect for life-saving tactile relief from x+y=?) Make sure that the uncoiled rope at your feet is not knotted or tangled before you start. Lay the working end in your right palm (end away from you) so that at least two feet of rope hangs down from your hand (#20a). Hold the rope in position with your right thumb. Grasp the standing part of the rope with your left hand and continuing to hold tight with the right thumb, pass your left hand to the full extent of that arm: this movement determines the size (top to bottom) of the coil. If you want the coil larger, extend both arms away from one another as the rope passes through the left hand. Place the formed coil into the palm of your right hand(#20b). Continue making coils and holding them

#20a

#20b

in the right hand until you approach the end of the rope. If you find that the coils begin to "figure-eight"; i.e., twist onto themselves to form a figure-eight pattern (#20c), take the twist out by turning the rope between the fingers and thumb of the left hand in a counterclockwise direction as you form each coil. If you don't care about twists in your coil, forget what I just said — some people care.

#20c

There you stand with all the coils in your right hand and about 6–8 feet of rope left uncoiled. Find the three-foot end that you started with and bend the working end back on itself to form an uncrossed loop. Lay that loop on top of the coils with the loop facing

#20d #20e

away from you (#20d). Take the 6–8 foot remaining length and begin to wrap it around the top of the coil so that each wrap is made neatly and tightly toward the end of the loop (#20e). When you have completed at least 8–10 wraps and you are beginning to run out of wrapping rope, reeve what remains of the working end through the loop (#20f). Your final move in

#20f #20g

this dramatic coiling scenario is a decisive one — find the end of the coiling rope (look for the colored tape) and pull it smartly so that the loop closes definitively and locks the working end in place (#20g). Not many knot sequences allow a final move that displays such a high degree of dynamic casual competence.

If you made your coils well and wrapped tightly, your coiling job will not only remain intact until the rope is used again, but, worn cross-chest, the coil will impart an Alpine aura that transcends unsuspected agoraphobia, and looks good in fairly spontaneous photographs. Don't forget to hold your hand in a palm-down position above your eyes (index finger juxtaposed to eyebrows), as you try to visually determine the best climbing line up whatever crag you're facing — there's more to looking good than simply coiling rope (#21).

#21

The purpose of coiling a rope (facetiousness temporarily aside) is to put the rope into a "package" that will allow easy carrying to the climbing site and also provide ease of deployment. A rope that is simply bundled together at the end of a program day will cause considerable wasted tangle-time when you attempt to use the rope again. Also, as you uncoil a rope prior to a day's use, the uncoiling sequence gives you an opportunity to quickly check the integrity of the rope's surface.

#22a

The Alpine coil that you just completed also provides a handy rescue function that is easy to implement. Take a look at the illustration showing a rescuer carrying a disabled person on his/her back (#22b). The coil, in this case, acts as a temporary backpack and facilitates the evacuation of a person who is not ambulatory because of minor injuries, e.g., sprained ankle. Adjust the size of the coil and positioning of the coil wraps to make the "backpack" arrangement functional and comfortable for you.

#22b

The Chainstitch Coil

There is no doubt that the results of this "coiling" technique produces an attractive piece of rope work (#23a). Aesthetics aside, chainstitching a rope is functional.

#23a

If your rope needs obvious cleaning as the result of a muddy caving trip or prolonged use in a gritty environment, chainstitch the rope before putting it into the washing machine (mild soap and cycle). So entwined, the rope will not spontaneously knot and kink, also allowing the soapy water to reach all parts of the rope. A chainstitched rope will also hang dry faster. **Do not machine dry your rope.**

Attach (tie) one end of your rope to a solid object or have someone hold an end. (If you double over your rope length before beginning, you will half your coiling time. The illustrations depict chainstitching with doubled rope/webbing.) About twelve inches from the end, fashion an overhand loop and pass a bight of the standing part through that loop. You have just tied a slip knot. A chainstitched rope represents a series of these slip knots tied one after another, so keep going. Continue bringing the standing part up and through the loop formed by the previous section of standing part. If you want the chainstitch to be tight (close knotting is convenient if you plan to carry the rope this way), pull each juxtaposed slip knot up firmly to the next one. If you need the stitching loose (better for washing), be more casual in the formation of each slip knot and the spacing between; like the rope illustration (#23b).

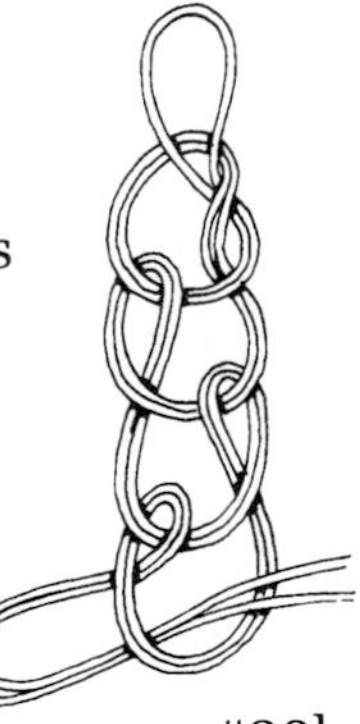

#23b

If you haven't discovered it already, when you pull on the working end, with the standing end made secure, the chainstitches (slip knots) dissolve one after another in a satisfying rapid-fire manner.

Chainstitching can be used just as effectively to "coil" sections of webbing. Find the center of the webbing length and

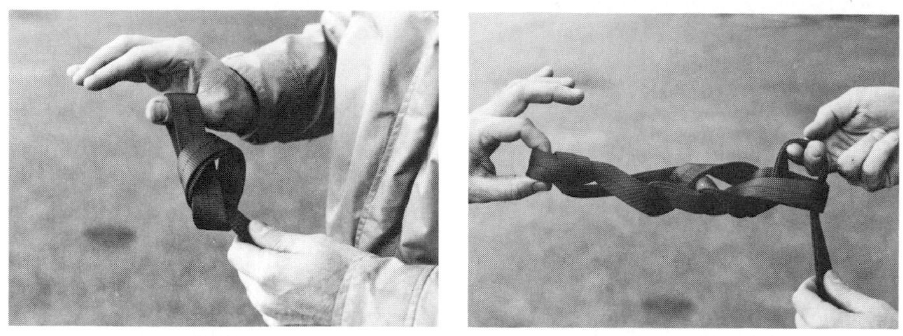

#24a #24b

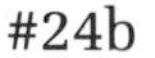

use that loop to tie an overhand loop (#24a). Reeve a double section of standing webbing from immediately below the overhand knot up and through the overhand loop, producing the first of many slip knots. Continue making slip knots as above, until you reach the end of the webbing. Reeve both loose ends of webbing through the final slip loop and pull tight (#24b). This will anchor your chain or sinnet. When you are ready to use the webbing again, remove the loose ends and pull them. The juxtaposed slip knots will satisfyingly dissolve in sequence until the original overhand loop is reached. Untie the overhand knot, and you're ready to go — I don't know where you are going, but at least you have a section of webbing ready to use when you get there.

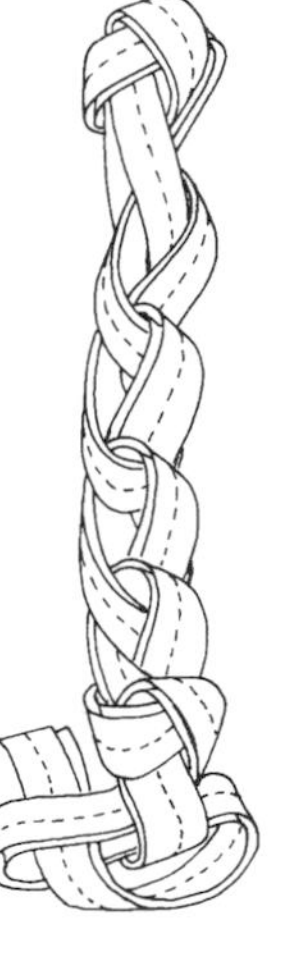

#24c

In some knot books, chainstitching is included under decorative knots (chain sinnet) and other authors include the sequence as a series of trick knots. Now you can use a touch of digital legerdemain to be tricky in a utilitarian way.

Cut and Burn

All ropes used on the modern ropes course, from rigging to belay use, are currently manufactured from synthetic materials — and if they aren't they should be. There is no reason to use natural fiber rope (manila, sisal, flax), unless you are setting up an historical diorama of what a ropes course used to look and sound like. Synthetic ropes are superior in every way, except they don't creak and squeak like the rat lines and rigging of *The Pequod* or *The Bounty.* Use 3/4" tarred Italian manila hemp for the Burma Bridge hand and foot lines if creaking and squeaking benefits your ropes course ambiance. (Firefighters have to use natural fiber rope in some circumstances because of nylon's low melting point.)

Cutting modern synthetic rope is considerably different from the old manila chop technique. Treated manila hemp was tough stuff and would dull a knife quick-time, so the most expedient way to cut through hard-lay manila was with a sharp hatchet and quick wrist. It was not necessary to tape the rope prior to this satisfying guillotine maneuver because the tight lay of the rope precluded formation of a cowstail. However, if you tried hacking through a piece of synthetic multiline, two world class cowstails would immediately remind you of your folly. Do this: chop all the manila you need to fulfill your cut and slash proclivities, but tape, cut, and burn synthetic ropes.

Using black, warm (cold tape is brittle) PVC electrician's tape, take 3–4 turns around the diameter of the rope to be cut. The tape should cover at least an inch of the rope's surface. Place the taped area on a cutting board and slice through the center of the tape with a sharp blade — dull knives are an abomination. A keen edge says something about its owner.

Entoning *flame on*, fire up a butane torch and "touch" the cut rope ends with the pencil tip flame in order to heat seal them. If you *touch* them too long the ends will become a bulbous mass of melted plastic that smells almost as bad as it looks. You need just a touch (2 secs. max.) to "glass" over a smoothly cut end.

Nothing else is needed to secure the end — sadly, the days of whipping rope are over. I whip a rope end occasionally just to remind myself that I can and because it looks good. There's not much image in a length of tape.

After you have experienced how quickly rope melts and burns, the admonition of ***NO SMOKING OR WELDING AROUND ROPES OR WEBBING*** makes a lot of sense.

Rope Types/Usage on Ropes Courses

The available choices of rope types and knots for different adventure curriculum needs can be confusing, particularly to a novice.

The simplistic solution is to choose one strong rope type, an equally effective hitch or bend, and use them exclusively for all applications. If you purchased a length of Skyline II rope, and learned how to tie a bowline knot, you could accomplish every installation task and climbing challenge on a ropes course, but such stubborn frugality is unnecessary, not functional, and often uncomfortable or even dangerous. Utilizing three or four knots and taking advantage of the advances in cordage engineering will increase your confidence and makes the use of rope seem more in tune with an activity, rather than struggling in spite of it.

People who work with rope learn by association the characteristics, specifications, and terminology of the cordage trade. Eventually an occupational vocabulary develops, but to an interested novice these esoteric words and references are confusing and frustrating. Refer to the glossary for some vernacular demystification and if you need further clarification of the information in this book, call the Project Adventure office at 508/468-7981. The information is free, the call isn't. (Notice — the first three digits are 508, not 800.)

If all this reading is giving you a headache and you yearn for a more mindless video approach, call or write Project Adventure for the 45-minute color video, *Karl on Knots*, a graphic and animated reminder of the rope and knot data that you need and which, coincidentally, nearly duplicates the material in this book. Hey, buy the whole package (book & video) and be the first on your block to throw a KNOT party. You know... tie a few image knots, laugh at the guy on the video trying to be serious, impress your date by threading-the-needle, tie each other up... heh heh !

Rope Types

Maxim

11mm diameter kernmantle
Average bowline tensile strength — 3,000 pounds
Estimated average tensile strength — 5,000 pounds
Static elongation — 6%

Maxim is the first American-made kernmantle rope to receive U.I.A.A. certification. The rope is designed primarily for rock climbing and is thus ideal for ropes course belay use.

Maxim is available in a variety of colors, it's reasonably priced, easy to work with, and holds a knot well. After you have experienced the handling characteristic of a kernmantle rope, it's hard to go back to three strand hawser-lay rope, e.g., Skyline II.

KM III

12mm diameter static kernmantle
Average bowline tensile strength — 5,000 pounds
Estimated average tensile strength — 8,300 pounds
Working elongation — 2% @ 450 pounds

KM III is a static kernmantle rope designed primarily for rescue operations. The rope features high tensile strength, low stretch, good abrasion resistance and displays little kinking tendencies when used as a single-line rappel rope.

Project Adventure uses KM III as a rappel rope because its diameter is slightly (1/16") larger than most standard climbing ropes. This hefty characteristic develops additional friction as the rope passes through a figure-8 descender, making single rope rappelling more comfortable.

KM III is also the rope of choice for the Flying Squirrel ropes course event, because of its static quality, great strength, abrasion resistance, and hands-on holdability.

Multiline

Multiline is a reduced-stretch 3-strand rope constructed with a polypropylene core, sheathed by polyester yarns. This rope, unlike manila hemp, feels good in the hand and is resistant to u/v and biological deterioration. Multiline is also easy to splice and, size for size, is much stronger than comparable natural fiber ropes.

Project Adventure installers use the various diameters of this rope as follows:

3/8" — (3,200 lbs. tensile) Herringbone cross ropes on the Burma Bridge. Periphery or framing rope for the Spider Web.

1/2" — (5,200 lbs. tensile) Tension hand ropes for the Tension Traverse. Trolley hand ropes.

5/8" — (7,500 lbs. tensile) Swing ropes for various events. Construction of Fidget, Firecracker, and rope ladders. Descent rope on the back of The Wall. Connector rope from a harness to the two-wheel zip pulley.

3/4" (9,800 lbs. tensile) — Parallel Kitten Crawl ropes. Commando Crawl rope. Vertical Playpen ropes.

1" (17,100 lbs. tensile) — 4-Way Tug-O-War Ropes. Swing to a regain.

Polypropylene

The lightest of all the synthetic ropes, "poly" will float in salt or fresh water. Poly has low elasticity and is highly resistant to chemicals. However, because of its polished slippery surface and u/v susceptibility, poly is not suited for most ropes course applications. The rope is identified by its bright yellow color and shiny surface.

Project Adventure uses polypropylene in the following diameters:

1/4" — (1,350 tensile) The boundary rope for constructing a Maze. The outline rope for the Unholy Alliance (4-Way Tug-O-War) and other games that need an inexpensive and easily seen boundary rope.

1/2" — (4,700 lbs. tensile) As a tension traverse rope over mud or water. For hand lines on the trolley.

Skyline II

11mm 3-strand hawser laid rope
Average bowline tensile strength — 3,600 pounds
Estimated average tensile strength — 6,000 lbs
Working elongation — 11% @ 500 lbs

Skyline II is a firmly laid, 3-strand mountain climbing rope that exhibits excellent abrasion resistance and good knot holding ability. Skyline II is not certified by the U.I.A.A. because of its comparatively high elasticity under strain, but the rope has met the impact force and dynamic fall requirements when U.I.A.A. tested.

If budget considerations suggest a lower priced but equally safe belay rope, Skyline II meets the requirements. This type of belay rope will generally last longer, with equal use, than kernmantle rope of the same diameter. Three-strand hawser-laid rope is easier to check for abrasion and cuts, but is not as easy to handle as kernmantle. If you can afford kernmantle, go for it; your staff will love you.

Knot Application

This is the section that provides some rationale for having learned all these hitches and bends. Knots are nice, but there has to be an occasional application other than a handmade gift-for-mom geegaw from adventure camp to stick on the refrigerator door (with a spliced-in magnet, and including a couple little filigreed hearts tied on with festoons of other fancy macramé-type stuff...)

The following knot and rope applications (hold the macramé) are those currently used by Project Adventure ropes course installers and by Project staff who teach ropes course technical skills.

Bowline-on-a-Bight

- To provide a loop for carabiner clip-in between the end of a belay rope and a harness (Swiss Seat; Studebaker Wrap).
- Split the two bowline loops and clip them separately into two harnesses for use on the Australian back-up belay.

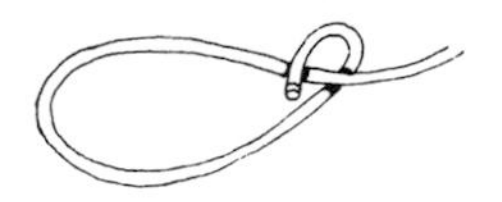

Butterfly Knot

- Wherever a non-slip knot is needed on the bight. Can take a considerable strain without jamming.

Bowline-on-a-Round-Turn

- Used wherever there will be considerable strain on the knot.

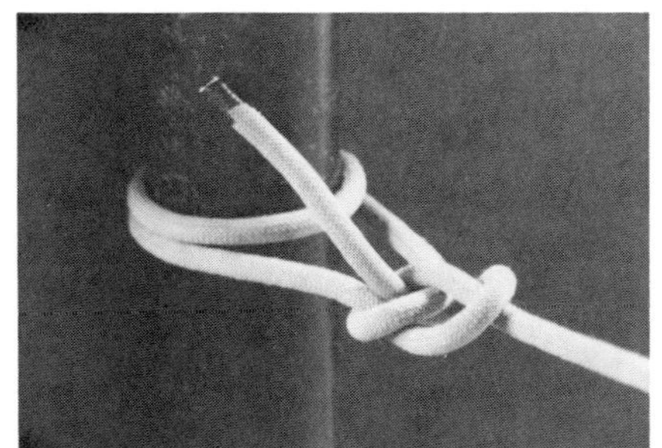

Figure Eight Loop

- An alternative to the Bowline-on-a-Bight, to provide a loop for carabiner clip-in between the end of a belay rope and a harness (Swiss Seat; Studebaker Wrap).

Safety or Tunnel Knot (Double Overhand)

- Used to back up any knot, bend or hitch that involves a person's safety.
- See photos of Bowline on-a-Bight and Figure Eight Loop.

Double Fisherman's Knot (Barrel Knot)

- To tie the ends of a sling together to serve as a prusik loop.
- To tie the ends of two belay ropes together for use as a double rappel rope.

Square Knot

- Used to finish off a Swiss Seat or Studebaker Wrap.

Killick Hitch

- Used to tie a section of #4 cord onto the working end of a belay rope.
- For dragging a heavy log. (Used in this context, the timber hitch replaces the clove hitch.)

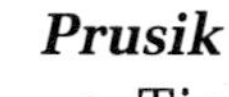

Prusik

- Tied with small diameter slings to allow ascending a vertically hung, larger diameter rope.
- Allows tightening/loosening of the Spider Web frame rope.
- Allows adjustment of the Kitten Crawl ropes.
- Similar adjustment of the Commando Crawl rope.
- Maintains tightness of the safety guide rope that protects participants on the Wall platform.

Eye Splice

- Used when a permanent eye is indicated in the end of a rope; e.g., zip wire connector rope; swing ropes; multi-vine ropes; tension traverse ropes. An eye spliced loop is considerably stronger than a loop fashioned from a knot.

Back Splice

- Whenever the end of a three strand rope needs to be finished off; e.g., end of a swing rope, tension traverse rope, trolley ropes, multi-vine ropes.

Glossary

"Even if it is advanced, keep it basic."

It's important for you to use and be comfortable with the accepted vernacular that is historically associated with rope and knots: cordage vocabulary establishes part of the image that enhances the trust in a student/instructor relationship. I'll admit that I occasionally encourage people to change the names and rules of games to promote a sense of player empowerment (Monopoly is one of my favorite time-honored games to "rearrange." I get out of jail free all the time and regularly collect more than $200.00 as I pass GO, cause I'm over 50 years old, etc.), but when it comes to hands-on technical skill, surround yourself with as much traditional image as you can establish. I mentioned this ploy earlier in the book — just a reminder.

average bowline tensile strength — The tensile strength of an unknotted rope is largely theoretical because to support or hold anything a rope must be knotted, thereby reducing the tensile strength. When a rope's strength is tested to destruction, bowline knots are usually tied in the rope ends for attachment to a hydraulic testing mechanism.

belay — The protection or protection system afforded by a safety line.

bend — Tying (knotting) the ends of two free ropes together. See knot.

bight — That part of the rope between the working end and the standing part.

breaking strength — The advertised tensile strength of a rope; i.e., the strain in pounds that causes a rope to break. Does not take into consideration shock loading or anything else that might weaken the rope.

bungee (bunji) cord — Also referred to as shock cord. Parallel lengths of rubber band material held in place by a woven cotton or nylon sheath (mantle) covering.

carabiner — A metal alloy snap-link device used by climbers as a substitute for a knot. Only carabiners with locking gates should be used on a ropes course.

cows tail (also Irish Pennant) — The frayed end of a rope, and half the title of a book on adventure curriculum.

destructive testing — Hydraulic pull tests performed on critical pieces of protective gear to determine ultimate tensile strength. Such tests result in the destruction of the tested piece. Great fun to watch.

dress up — To insure that the strands that make up the knot are lying true and not crossed over one another. To neglect dressing a knot may result in a reduction of knot strength.

dynamic belay — A belay system that has a considerable amount of give; trees bending, rope stretching, controlled release of rope, etc.

eye — A loop made in the end of a rope by use of knots or more functionally by splicing.

fid — A conical tool that is used to make splicing easier. The classic fid is a solid carrot-like tool made of wood. The modern fid is made with a wood handle and an attached grooved piece of stainless steel.

figure eight — Either a knot arrangement or a mechanical belay/ rappel device.

flake — A single turn in a coil.

Goldilock's rule — Not too long, and not too short, but *just right.*

hawser lay — A generic rope type characterized by a spiral/ twisted configuration of strands, e.g., Skyline II

hitch — A hitch fastens a rope to a solid object or to another rope, which takes no part in the actual knotting.

kernmantle — A generic term for high quality synthetic rope that has parallel and twisted interior nylon fibers (kern), contained within a woven exterior covering (mantle).

Killick hitch — Strictly, a timber hitch and half hitch in combination, used for hauling cylindrical objects (logs). In this book, also refers to a clove hitch and half hitch used together.

knot — A knot is a *knot* when the manipulation is performed in the end(s) of the rope. See bend. According to Clifford Ashley, "Any complication in rope except accidental ones."

loop — A turn of the rope that crosses itself. Can be an overhand or underhand loop depending upon its orientation to the person forming the loop.

natural fiber rope — All rope made from natural organic fibers, e.g., manila hemp, sisal, flax.

number 4 cord — Small diameter nylon cord used for hauling belay ropes up and through shear-reduction belay devices. Also called *lazy line.*

overkill — A term inappropriately used to indicate superfluous use of an extremely strong section of rope or piece of gear. Try, *over-engineered,* or, as a structural engineer corrected me recently, try *properly engineered.*

ROSA — **R**eally **O**utstanding **S**afety **A**ttachments. Safety products produced by Project Adventure, Inc. that are specific to ropes course use.

rapid link — A link resembling a carabiner, but with an open/close screw gate. Rapid links are less expensive and considerably stronger than carabiners, but they are also heavier and less convenient to use.

rappel — A self-controlled slide down an anchored rope. *Abseil* is the German/Swiss word for this activity. Rappelling is spelled with two L's.

retired rope — Rope that has been used as belay line, but which has been removed from service for a variety of reasons — excessive wear, ultra-violet deterioration, external abrasions or cuts, peace-of-mind, etc. Retired rope should not be used for any purpose that involves an individual's safety.

round-turn — A turn of the rope taken around a solid object to relieve strain on the knot, e.g., Bowline-on-a-round-turn.

safe working load (SWL) — The estimated load that a rope can sustain, taking into account those factors that can weaken the rope; knot type, rope shear, age of the rope, shock loading, etc. Usually factored at 20% of the tensile strength.

seize — A lashing for holding two ropes or parts of rope together.

setting a knot — To tighten all parts of the knot equally.

SR Block (shear reduction device) — A **ROSA** safety product, developed by K. Rohnke and P. Rosa for Project Adventure, Inc., that reduces the amount of shear applied to a belay rope.

shear — The tension and friction produced in a rope as it passes over a small diameter object under pressure, e.g., over a single carabiner. Shear can reduce the tensile strength of a rope as much as 50%.

shock loading — A kinetic load applied to a rope, cable, eye bolt, etc. Falling off a ropes course element applies a shock load to the rope.

slash rope — Retired sections of rope. Not to be used programmatically for anything that involves an individual's safety.

sling rope — A generic term referring to a length of rope used for tying a Swiss seat or Studebaker wrap.

S/S Pulley — Performs essentially the same shear reduction function as the SR Block. Produced and developed by Project Adventure, Inc.

standing end— The opposite of the working end of the rope.

standing part — That part of the rope not considered an end and not being handled or worked.

static rope — Rope which exhibits little or negligible stretch.

static belay — A belay set-up characterized by a rope running from an anchor point directly to the climber. There is not much give in a static belay nor does it allow easy retrieval of a fallen climber.

sticht plate — A mechanical belay device that is efficient and easy to use.

synthetic rope — Rope manufactured from synthetic fibers; not made from organic material, e.g., multiline, kernmantle, polypropylene.

tuber — A mechanical belay device that is efficient and easy to use.

U.I.A.A. — Union of International Alpine Associations (a fairly accurate translation from the french). A European organization that maintains quality control testing of Alpine gear.

whoops — Contra-indicated exclamation when working with knots and safety gear. Anticipate pejorative connotations when followed by *Uh-Oh.*

working end — That end of the rope used for tying a knot. Opposes the standing end.

zymurgy — The science of brewing — you should know something about this...

Index